THE BUZZ ON™

XTREME SPORTS

Tom Reynolds

Dale Kiefer

LF LEBHAR-FRIEDMAN BOOKS

NEW YORK · CHICAGO · LOS ANGELES · LONDON · PARIS · TOKYO

The Buzz On Xtreme Sports

Lebhar-Friedman Books
425 Park Avenue
New York, NY 10022

Published by Lebhar-Friedman Books
Lebhar-Friedman Books is a company of Lebhar-Friedman, Inc.

Printed in the United States of America

Library of Congress Cataloging in Publication Data on file at the Library of Congress

ISBN: 0-86730-848-6

Produced by Progressive Publishing (1-888-355-8044) (www.propubltd.com)
Editor: John Craddock; Creative Director: Nancy Lycan
Art Directors: Nancy Lycan, Michele Thomareas
Editorial Contributors: John Craddock III, Paul Love
Design Director: Vivian Torres; Designers: Angela Connolly, Marco Echevarria, Lanette Fitzpatrick, Suzanne Miller, Rena Seibert, Vivian Torres, David Womble, Peter Royland

Visit our Web site at lfbooks.com

Volume Discounts
This book makes a great gift and incentive. Call (212) 756-5206 for information on volume discounts

Disclaimer: Every effort has been taken to ensure the accuracy of the information given in this book. No liability can be accepted by the authors or publisher for any loss, damage, or injury, either through errors or omissions or by following the advice in this book. Do not attempt these activities without professional supervision.

THE BUZZ ON™

XTREME SPORTS

ACKNOWLEDGMENTS

The authors dutifully wish to thank the following contributors:

Stephanie Barton, Amy Blackwell, Robert M. Brink, Jim Eagen, Jeff Eyamie, Candice Livingston, Amy Lewis Marquis, Sean McCoy, and Genevieve Thiers.

Author Tom Reynolds wishes to thank his mom, "who was wise to tell me to work hard, kind to show me how, and supportive when it actually got tough."

Author Dale Kiefer would like to thank his parents, Carol and Charlie Kiefer, for instilling in him an abiding love of the written word; his friend and mentor, author Mary Ann Taylor-Hall, for inspiring him to follow his muse; his wife Bonnie for her unflagging support and encouragement, and his sons, Nathan and Adam, for their unconditional love.

CONTENTS

XTREME SPORTS— BEFORE & AFTER

The history of Xtreme sports can be divided into two parts: There's everything that happened before 1995 and everything after.

Some Xtreme sports actually have ancient roots. Bungee jumping dates back to prehistoric societies. Many Xtreme sports can trace their origins back to a single source—surfing. Polynesians and South Pacific islanders were gliding across waves way before Columbus bumped into land. And before the Beach Boys, Frankie, or Annette made a quick buck from the sand and surf scene, the Hawaiians knew how special the sport was—only nobility was allowed to surf.

Skateboarding itself sprang from bummed surfers looking for action when the waves wouldn't cooperate. In the suburban sprawl that was beginning to dominate the Southern California area, there were plenty of places to "sidewalk surf." Broken scooters from the 1950s eventually were transformed into boards with better rubber wheels and high performance potential.

While skateboarding has ebbed and flowed in popularity, at its core are the main attractions for the early Xtreme fanatics. You don't need a beach, a river, or a mountain. Any smooth stretch of concrete or asphalt works fine. And it's an "alternative sport." Basketball only allows so much expression. Creativity in football is almost non-existent. Baseball? Please. Xtreme sports shout "me." They yell "thrill." They have the neighbors wondering, "What the hell is that guy doing?"

MAKING OF THE
X GAMES

A SPORTS REVOLUTION

New Xtreme sports evolved in their own mutant way. From skateboards came other variations such as street luge and in-line skating. In the late 1970s street luging spread like an underground fungus. It developed a cult-like following as people streaked down the hills of Southern California and Washington, often under the cover of night, blazing down winding roads, inches from the ground. Not surprisingly, many crashed, and a few were seriously hurt. From these night flights came the Signal Hill Rules, guidelines that first established requirements for boards, wheels, and safety. The attraction for luge racers was simple: Where else can you go so fast that the wheels of your board actually liquefy, beneath you? Sounds like fun, huh?

In-line skating traces its popularity to a couple of hockey players looking for a way to train in the summer. These Minnesota guys made adjustments to the wheels and brake system on some skates, and have since been widely credited with what we now consider in-line skates. From there, in-liners began taking their show to ramps and terrain parks once ruled only by boarders, who were none too happy to share. The in-liners didn't back down. With endless lip grinds and fearless flips, in-liners took the world of traditional roller skating and literally turned it upside down.

Other sports under the Xtreme sports umbrella still remain out of the mainstream. Ask anyone involved in whitewater kayaking or rock climbing his opinion, and you're likely to hear the same answer: He doesn't do it for the spotlight. Ever since there have been mountains there have been men and women born with a need to climb. In 1924, when asked why he wanted to scale Mount Everest, perhaps the most inhospitable place on earth, George Leigh Mallory gave an answer for the ages: "Because it is there." Every Xtreme athlete can relate.

For others, rather than reaching a pinnacle and enjoying the view, they prefer taking a flying leap when they hit the top. BASE (Building, Antenna, Span, and Earth) jumpers like their thrills short and swift. Then there are their slightly less insane skydiving and skysurfing cousins that at least use an airplane before they bail.

But nothing, absolutely nada, has had as dramatic an impact on the popularity of Xtreme sports as ESPN's X Games. Almost single-handedly, ESPN has ollied skating, freestyle BMX, and countless other life-and-limb threatening sports into people's living rooms and popular consciousness.

What started as an alternative-sports Olympics has spawned the Winter X Games, the Asian X Games, and numerous qualifying competitions such as the X Trials. It also has turned guys like Tony Hawk and Mat Hoffman into international celebrities with their own equipment franchises, video games, and swimming pools full of cash.

It all started in 1993, when ESPN gave a team of programmers the task of producing a worldwide competition for "alternative" sports. ESPN, and especially ESPN2, had carried skateboard competitions, freestyle BMX, street luge, and other alternative sports competitions for years. Most of those sports were shown on late-night television, when their perceived demographic (college students and people who work at the mall) could catch them over beer and a pizza.

But it didn't take a programming genius to figure out that a massive surge in mountain bike sales might be accompanied by an equivalent surge in people wanting to watch mountain bike competitions. Somebody at ESPN latched on, and in April 1994, the first Extreme Games (as they were originally called—this was later changed to X Games so that foreign advertisers would have an easier time translating the name) were announced. They were set for June 1995 in that Xtreme sports hotbed of—Rhode Island. (Rhode Island?)

Yep, ESPN's marketing geniuses had scoured the country looking for the perfect place to have their inaugural competition, and settled on a lesser known, but friendly section of Providence, Rhode Island, near the Brown University and Rhode Island School of Design campuses. College Hill, one of the local landmarks, would provide the street luge and in-line skating venues, while other competitions would be held in nearby Middletown, and Mount Snow, Vermont. Sure, there were more BMX riders in California, but the collegiate atmosphere, proximity of water and hills, and the willingness of the community to take a gamble on the project was enough to give the Extreme Games liftoff. And did it ever take off. Over the seven-day run, from June 24 to July 1, 1995, 198,000 spectators attended the games while millions watched the broadcasts.

It was not what everyone expected, however. While the televised broadcasts were incredibly fast paced with techno music and slick graphics, spectators at the street luge complained that a pilot and his luge would only be visible for two or three seconds (as they zipped by at 60 mph) with 15 minutes of lag time between runs. Not the sort of thing that keeps people clamoring for more.

Also, while the majority of the skaters and others interested in the games were younger, sponsors were surprised to find that the majority of the athletes were in their mid-twenties to early forties. It quickly became apparent that in order to become a world-class wake boarder, you needed access to a ski boat. Bungee jumpers needed their own harnesses and bungees. Climbers needed their own gear. Likewise, high-end mountain bikes are pricey. The average teenager didn't have a big enough allowance to cover that sort of investment. Plus, as one athlete quipped: "We're older… because most parents don't let their kids do what we do."

The extraordinary popularity of the X Games (the name was officially changed in 1996) attracted sponsors in droves. This filtered down to small, local competitions, where a young athlete might have an opportunity to win some cash or some gear that would put him on the road to the big leagues. With sponsorships from the likes of Chevy, Nike, AT&T, Miller, and other big names, the trickle-down effect would have made any Republican economist proud.

In 1996 the games were again held in Rhode Island, drawing a crowd of 200,000, and the first Winter X Games were announced, though it would not debut until 1997. While the Winter X Games failed to draw near the numbers of the X Games (the inaugural year saw only 38,000 spectators), it was wildly popular in broadcast, and was watched in 198 countries in 21 languages.

Summer 1997 saw the games move to Oceanside and San Diego, California, strongholds for Xtreme sports athletes. Meanwhile, ESPN had been building a worldwide publicity fervor, with international exhibitions and tours from Shanghai, China, to Disneyland in Paris.

The year 1999 was a big one for the X Games. Attendance in Oceanside/San Diego topped 275,000 fans, and was highlighted by Tony Hawk's now-famous 900-degree skateboard aerial. (It also marked the announcement of the Winter X Games' move from its home in Crested Butte, Colorado, where it had attracted dismal crowds of only 25,000 to 30,000 for both the '97 and '98 events.) The overall popularity of the X Games increased worldwide in 1999, spurred by the international exhibitions and broadcast saturation.

The year 2000 marked the Winter X Games' major leap, as nearly 84,000 fans journeyed to Mount Snow, Vermont to see the outrageous display of big-air snowboarding and X-skiing. The winter games are scheduled to stay on the East Coast, while the flagship games will leave California for Philadelphia in 2002.

The events of the X Games have evolved since its initial broadcast. Kiteskiing, wind surfing, and mountain biking were dropped and wakeboarding was added. The current X Games roster is composed of skateboarding, BMX, motocross, in-line skating, climbing, street luge, and wakeboarding, with various sub-competitions in each of the major divisions. (For the winter games, the lineup currently is motocross, X-skiing, snocross, snowboarding, and ultracross.)

ESPN promises that if a sport becomes too mainstream, it will axe it just as it did mountain biking in 1996. More cynical pundits suggest that if a sport becomes popular enough to generate its own revenue stream, ESPN will spin it off into a separate broadcast and move a new sport into the X Games spotlight. But change is the hallmark of alternative sports, and the athletes and fans both admire the fresh attitude and a commitment to emphasizing the "alternative" in alternative sports that has made the X Games the Xtreme sports standard.

1 YOU'RE GROUNDED!

There's something about asphalt that cries out: "Put wheels on any thing you can find and come cruise on me. I dare you." You can't resist that challenge, and you become bolder with every ride. From skateboarding to in-line skating to street luge, the faster the asphalt zooms by and the closer your body is to it, the better. Even when the pavement scrapes your skin or breaks your bones, you worship those injuries, all in the name of the almighty thrill. They are badges of honor.

But there's a way you can save yourself some major bumps. Take a little time to read about the basics of Xtreme sports that rely on wheels and pavement—plus a few pints of plasma. What looks so simple that any street punk can do it will take on a new degree of difficulty you might never have imagined. Know the top speeds a street luge hits? More than 90 mph, so be prepared—or else.

SKATEBOARDING

Skateboarding has for years suffered an image problem, at least to outsiders: Skaters were viewed as bad seeds. Old ladies and policemen would frown as boarders cruised past them. Mom grabbed Little Johnny and asked why he didn't just play baseball like a normal kid. The answer?

It's all about the thrill, Mom.

Whether you're cruising along inches from the sidewalk, or launching from a ramp and twisting through the air, skateboarding is all about the juice. And it has been since its early days, when boards were nothing more than modified scooters. Eventually, manufacturers began to design and create boards specifically for skaters, ones that turned and carved, boards with special wheels and moving parts that gave a rider better control.

Since the early days in California's San Fernando Valley—believed by many to be the Garden of Eden of the sport—skateboarding has seen more ups and downs than Kenny on *South Park*. The booms and, more so, the busts, that skateboarding has endured show that the grandfather of Xtreme sports is healthy and is not going anywhere any time soon.

Sorry, Mom.

THE PARTS

Understanding what you are riding will help your overall performance once you master the basics. A skateboard, despite the years of development and the introduction of modern advances, is not too far removed from its scooter ancestor. It's basically still made up of four main components:

1. A deck
2. A pair of trucks
3. Wheels
4. Bearings

That's it, really. There are some other accessories that riders may choose to use, but these are the basics.

You can figure out what most of those pieces are, but here is a quick tutorial, just in case:

• The deck is the main part of the board. It's constructed of thin wood layers and usually has some flex to aid in landing jumps. Modern decks also sport different curves on specific parts of the board that help the rider pull off various tricks and turns. Decks can also differ in length and width.

• Trucks are a crucial element of a skateboard. They connect the wheels to the deck and transfer a rider's weight in the turns. Having a good metal pair of trucks is necessary. Along with bearing the brunt force of hard landings, trucks also double as a nice grinding area for skilled riders.

• Everyone knows the wheels, but there are variations within this broad category. Made of urethane, a type of plastic, wheels come in different sizes and degrees of hardness. Softer wheels give smoother rides, while harder wheels offer riders more speed. Smaller wheels let riders turn better, and bigger wheels are suited for cruising since they provide speed over longer distances.

• Bearings are the misunderstood child in the skateboard family because beginners, and even some experienced riders, don't really know what they do. Located inside the wheel, they are the round metal balls that allow the wheels to spin on the trucks. Got it? Each bearing has a rating that basically tells how well it will spin. A helpful reminder when buying bearings is: The higher the rating (known as an ABEC) the faster the bearing. As Fletch once said, "Maybe you boys need a refresher course. It's all ball bearings nowadays!"

THE DANGER IS FUN

It takes a certain mindset—many say being crazy helps—to stand on a moving board, hurtle down hills and over ramps for *fun*! But the risk factor is definitely a draw for most riders. Taking certain precautions, though, can save skaters countless hours in recovery, along with hundreds of dollars in Band-Aids. For the record, skateboarding is a dangerous sport. Not even pros ride without some sort of protective equipment. Almost all skate parks in the country require riders to don kneepads, elbow pads, and a helmet to prevent any bruises to the melon. But if you're serious about riding, you will see some of your own blood from time to time. A scrape here, a nice road rash there— just get used to it. Minor damage is part of the sport. For extra defense, sport wrist guards when riding, wear long shirts and pants when the weather allows, and, more important, use your brain. Being smart can prevent most injuries.

THE ZEN OF RIDING (WITHOUT MOVING)

STANCE

Stance is the absolute first thing you need to learn. You take either one of two stances: goofy foot (right foot forward) or regular foot (left foot forward). An easy way to tell which one suits you is to simply stand on your board (preferably without rolling; try it on a carpet) without even thinking about it. Just get on it however it feels most comfortable. Chances are your instincts will put you in your proper stance. It's important to note that you want your feet to be almost sideways across the entire width of the board. You may feel a little more comfortable if you stand on the balls of your feet, with your heels hanging slightly off the side of the board. Feel how the board is shaped and test the flex of the trucks. Pretty easy, right? Enjoy it while it lasts, because that is the easiest it is ever going to get.

Since you are just standing still (and falling now would be pathetic), work on the stance you'll use after you put the wheels in motion. Also work on bending your knees and balancing your arms out to the side. (Note on coolness: *Do not* flap your arms as if you are preparing for take-off. Just keep them slightly stretched and relaxed. They are for balance, not for flight. So keep the flailing to a minimum. Even if you don't know how to skate yet, you can still save some self-respect by at least looking cool.)

Feet placement is critical in skateboarding once you advance beyond the basic skills. So get into the good habit of knowing where your feet are on the board at all times. You may need to peek down for a quick check when first starting out, but you'll quickly learn how to set your shoes judging by feel alone.

ON A ROLL

At this point, you should know your new board better than some of your strange relatives. With your protective gear on (especially a helmet), find a flat stretch of smooth asphalt. Parking lots and empty basketball courts are two ideal spots. The object here is to work on "The Push."

PUSHing

Stand on your board. Leave your front foot on the board, but point your toe toward the nose (front) a bit more than your usual stance, while slightly bending your front knee and stiffening up your leg a little (it will be supporting most of your body weight in a second). At this point you want to move your back foot off the side of the board (in the direction that your toe was pointing, never behind you),

When learning, keep a wide stance. The wider the distance between your feet, the more you spread your body's weight and the better balance you'll have. Wider is better, which is good in skating stances, but bad in bikini bottoms. A good rule of thumb is to keep your sneakers planted over the two trucks at either end of the board.

and push off of the ground with the ball of your foot. You should now be rolling and, hopefully, balanced on your front leg. From here you can either push again for more speed or return your foot to its position on the tail (back) of the board. When both feet are on the board, it is best to return them to their sideways position, as described in the stance section. This will help for when you need to turn. **Warning:** If you feel the urge, or if it feels more comfortable to use your front foot to push rather than your back foot—this means you should switch your stance. Do not learn to push with your front foot! This method is called "mongo foot," and people will laugh at you—a lot. If you think the name sounds ridiculous, wait until you see an uninformed, unfortunate soul applying this technique—it is even worse. Not to mention it makes setting up for tricks a lot more difficult.

STOP

You'll quickly realize, either thanks to an oncoming car or a telephone pole planted in your path, that skateboards have no built-in brakes. So while stopping on a dime is out, you do have some options:

• You can always bail. Rarely do skaters go so fast that they can't "run-out" a trick or a ride. Simply step off the board and keep your feet moving once you hit the ground so you don't face plant.

• With some experience, you can drag the tail of your board on the ground as you are riding and that will gradually slow you down. Not recommended for sudden stops (like the one needed to avoid a car or telephone pole).

• Using your back foot, you can also trail the toe of

your shoe off the side of the board. This is another way to gradually stop. It's also a swift way to ruin a good pair of sneakers.

FALL OUT

Stopping leads right into the art of falling. Skaters of every level fall all the time. Just like getting a few scrapes, it's part of the sport. And there is a right way and a wrong way to fall.

First: The wrong way. Instinct tells us to extend our arms to break our fall. What's more likely to happen is you'll end up breaking a wrist, even when wearing wrist guards. This is one of the most common injuries in the sport for that exact reason. Your puny wrists were not created to withstand the full weight of your body. In that contest, wrists lose out every time. Instead, riders should try to roll into a ball when they are headed for the ground. Even better, if a skater is wearing kneepads, he should knee slide; he'll probably walk away from any spill without a scratch.

TURNING

Turning is fairly simple. While moving, simply lean to your toes or your heels (depending on which way you want to turn). Use your ankles and lower legs to do so. If you use too much of your upper body for leaning, you will start looking like the Leaning Tower of Pisa, then lose your balance, and fall.

Another way to turn, which is a little more difficult, is called tick-tacking. This is simply leaning your weight to the tail of the board, slightly lifting the front wheels off of the ground, aiming the board in the direction you want to turn, and returning the front wheels back to the ground. Keep your front foot in its usual position and use it as a guide and a stabilizer. This will prevent you from flying backward and cracking your dome. The thought of being on only two wheels may seem scary at first, but you will get the hang of it quickly, and learning this will benefit every other move you will

try, especially if you come out of any given trick a little off balance. Turning this way will spare you a lot of unnecessary agony.

KING OF THE HILL

Why push when you can get some help from gravity? Excellent question. After the push comes the hill. If you are like most skaters, you have had a hill in mind from the minute you saw a skateboard. The thrill of speed, racing down an incline just inches above the concrete, can be like a drug. You'll want more after each run. You'll find yourself testing your limits and pushing your skills further each day. But at first, start small.

Your run should be a gradual smooth slope with a flat stretch at the bottom. (There should be no reason to say this, but we will anyway: *Avoid all traffic!*) As you start down, turning will be first on the assignment sheet. Turning, also called carving, is a way to control your speed. Work on linking together a series of turns that roughly resembles an S-pattern. Remember, keep your knees bent and arms out for balance.

ALL THE WORLD'S A RAMP

While street skating is only one facet of the sport, many urban riders have turned the style into an art. It may help to think of these guys and girls as the visionaries of the sport. While an average passerby sees a pretty fountain, a skilled skater sees the opportunity for a long boardslide. Trendy sculpture in the park? The urban rider sees a ramp off of which to launch. These skaters have a different perception of the world around them. And they say skateboarding isn't an art?

THE TRICKS

Street skating involves just that—the street and whatever obstacles you can find while you are on it. Curbs, sidewalks, benches, stairs, hand railings, other humans, you name it. With a little imagination, all are fair game for a potential skateboard playground. The main reason street skating is so very popular is because it is easily accessible. Almost anyone can go out his front door and find some smooth pavement and a curb or some

Ask anyone who rides a skateboard, and he will tell you the same thing. Most people are perplexed by the idea of being able to jump up a curb, or a bench, over a garbage can, or down some stairs on a skateboard by using only your feet and physics. When you learn to do so, you will then be the envy of your neighborhood, and you will have to explain to people who can't believe what they saw, exactly how you did it.

Start with your normal stance, with your back foot (using the ball of your foot) on the tail and your front foot a little more toward the center of the board than normal, rather than over the front bolts (the trucks), as in the regular stance. What you are going to do (preferably in one fluid motion) is crouch down slightly by bending and compressing your back and knees. Next, press the tail of the board down to the ground as hard as you can. As the tail hits the ground you need to slide your front foot up from the middle to the nose of the board while pulling up your back leg as high as you can. It is a lot to execute all at once. The goal here is to use the momentum of the tail rebounding from the ground combined with jumping to get the wheels in the air. The sliding of the front foot will then level the board out once you are off of the ground, so that you land back on all four wheels at once. Got it? Probably not, so keep trying until you do. An ollie is usually best learned on a new living room carpet or on your freshly mowed lawn—while you're stationary. Once you find that you can get yourself up in the air, try it while rolling, then over a 2x4, up a curb, over your girlfriend, etc. Ollieing is a technique that continually improves over time. As

stairs. If you are lucky you may have a skatepark nearby or a friend with a ramp or two. But don't get too far ahead of yourself, and don't even think about getting on a ramp at this point. First you must learn the basics or you will find yourself wearing a cast, missing some teeth, limping, or getting stitches. The tricks mentioned here must be learned before you even look at a ramp of any kind.

MEET OLLIE

The foundation of all skateboarding tricks is the ollie. The ollie is simply a "jump" on your skateboard. It will take you longer to learn than any other trick will.

you progress, your ability to ollie higher will improve as well. The world-record for the highest ollie is 45.5 inches (almost four feet!), and was set by professional skateboarder Danny Wainright.

GRINDING AND SLIDING

Once you are confident with your ollie ability, you can move on to a few of the basic curb tricks. These tricks can then be applied to benches, ledges, hand railings—whatever. A grind is basically just ollieing onto the corner of a curb and rolling, but using the metal surface of your trucks instead of riding on your wheels. The basic grind is pretty self-explanatory. You'll want to roll almost completely parallel to the curb (approach it at a slight angle), about four or five inches away from it.

Next, try to pop a level ollie, using your speed and the slight angle at which you are rolling, shift your weight, and aim your board for the corner of the curb. This may seem difficult, but you will be surprised at how easy getting into a grind is if you just picture aiming your feet where you want the trucks to land, because your feet should be positioned over the trucks

anyway. Once your trucks make contact, stiffen your legs a little and lean back. This will keep your forward momentum going and prevent your trucks from sticking to the cement. Now that you are grinding, try to look stylish and suave—this is essential in the ultra-cool world of skateboarding. Keep your legs stiff until you are ready to pop out of the grind. To get out, simply lift your front wheels as you would with the tick-tack mentioned earlier. Your back wheels should follow and you are now rolling away on the pavement—your degree of "extreme" exceeds where you were a few seconds ago. The number of different grinds that can be done is limitless. So get creative and don't limit yourself to just this one kind.

Slides are similar to grinds in the way they are executed. The only difference is that you are sliding on the curb with the surface of your nose, tail, or the center of the board between your trucks. The basic "rail slide" is done on the center of your board. To do this, approach the curb the same as you would for a grind, but instead of doing an ollie, just lift up your front wheels and turn your board perpendicular to the curb. Try to get the front truck over the corner of the curb and land the center of the board there instead. This

should lift your back wheels off the ground. Stiffen your legs, stand up straight with your weight back a tad, and hopefully you are sliding. Slide as far as you can. Hopefully you are wearing some cool clothes and your hair isn't messed up. To get off, simply lean your weight to the tail so your back wheels get back to the ground. When they do, pivot your board away from the curb and roll away.

FOUR TRICKS EVERY SKATER NEEDS TO KNOW

Watching a skate video or a pro contest can be demoralizing for a beginner. Here are some of the best riders in the world throwing the biggest airs, the sickest grabs, and the most amazing spins. You're likely to think that they all have superpowers, and that none of that is possible for a mere human like you. And that's where you're wrong.

Granted, those guys are the best. And yes, most have been riding since they could tie their own shoes. But almost every trick begins with the fundamentals. Master these and you can start building your own repertoire of moves. You may even have your own video someday.

THE KICKTURN

Less a trick than a fundamental move, the kickturn is all about necessity.

Technique – With your rear foot on the tail, press your weight down so as to bring the nose of the board off the ground. Then, with the front wheels in the air, swing your body in one direction to move the board. This can help in turning at sharper angles rather than relying on leaning into turns. After the wheels touch down, you can repeat the process in the opposite direction. Stylish freestyle riders can often spin around on the rear wheels to do complete rotations and more.

THE KICKFLIP

Don't you love when the name says everything about a trick? In a kickflip, you do just that: you kick the board and you flip it.

Technique – Take the same stance you would as if you were performing an ollie. The only real modification is rather than having your front foot placed over the center of the board, place it closer to the heel-side edge. Now, go through the same motions as in an ollie. As the board leaves the ground, move your front foot forward while tapping down on the edge to flip the board over. Lift your knees high so the board can rotate without any problem. Watch your landing and position your feet over the trucks on each end of the deck.

THE BOARDSLIDE

Perhaps one of the classier moves in skating, the boardslide is a true demonstration of a rider's balance and skill.

Technique – On the approach to a low rail or smooth edge, it is important to judge the right speed. When you get close, ollie the board off the ground and spin it so the rail sits directly below the center of the board. Have your feet spread wide toward the nose and tail of the deck to help with balance. Skaters can either ride the entire rail, or kick the tail to get the board back to the ground. There are different variations on the boardslide, too. Riders can opt to slide on the nose, the tail, or to grind the two trucks along an edge. But the fundamentals for getting to that spot are the same. The trick, as the name implies, is simply sliding the bottom of the board across a surface.

THE BACKSIDE AIR

Leaving the safety of the ground is a thrilling experience. It's even better when you nail the landing.

Once you feel comfortable enough on the street, find yourself a ramp and give this one a shot. It's literally a jump with a twist.

Technique – The backside air, aptly named because your back is toward the ramp in the air, is easier than its frontside cousin because it allows the rider to see the landing the entire time he or she is in the air. Depending on your speed (more speed equals bigger air), you may or may not have to do an ollie at the top of the ramp. If yes, then just go back to the fundamentals and nail an ollie right before reaching the top. If not, just let your speed take you into flight. In the air, it may help to reach behind you and grab the board with your front hand about midway down the rail. This will ensure you and your board both end up in the same place. At the peak of your jump, rotate your upper body around so that your front foot is not heading down the ramp. Let go of the board when you are about to land, keep your knees bent and have your weight over your front foot, going with the flow. Now you're ready to go for some bigger moves.

THE NEXT GENERATION

It is said that imitation is the sincerest form of flattery. It is also the best way to learn new tricks. After you master the moves above (and it will take a while, trust us), go hang at the local skatepark and watch the more experienced riders. Check out the latest videos and magazines, both of which are full of tips and pointers. But most of all, just skate. Tricks had to come from somewhere. Most likely they started with some guy or girl saying, "Hmm, I wonder if I can do this?" And you can too. So go do it.

A DAY AT THE PARK

In the hopes of making the world safer for skaters and pedestrians alike, designated skate parks have continued to grow since the first ones were created in the late 1970s. These havens allow riders to worry less than when on the street, while at the same time letting them maximize their skill, thanks in part to the special setups of ramps, rails, and bowls. A versatile skater can take his talents from the street curbs into the giant parks, while also ruling the backyard half-pipe. (Also see "Park It," page 34.)

MacDonald dazzles judges with tricks that are technically flawless. He has precision befitting a surgeon. On the next run, he will take a worn-out move and add his own spice to it, proving again that old dogs and new tricks do mix together well.

"I try to touch on all the bases," MacDonald said in an interview with SoulGear.com. "I have a more technical style with a bunch of trick combinations. A little of everything. Go big, 540, lip tricks, etc. I think that's what judges should be looking for."

But it's not just the kickflips that have propelled Big Mac to the apex of skating. Along with his talent comes a natural charisma that draws others to him. He's magnetic. That's a helpful quality for the skater crowned heir apparent to the sport's most famous rider, Tony Hawk. Throughout the years, Hawk and MacDonald often traded positions atop the winner's podium. In the past they have teamed up to win the doubles vert contest at the annual ESPN X Games. But Hawk has slowly begun to slide away from the sport, opening a gap most in the industry expect MacDonald to fill. And he has plans. Even as the gold medals continue to come, MacDonald has a fixed eye on continuing to elevate his sport. Although skateboarding is enjoying its greatest popularity ever, MacDonald is a visionary and sees more.

"The next level is to have a skateboard park next to every basketball court in this country," MacDonald said.

The big man has big plans, so don't write him off too soon. MacDonald has a few more runs that are sure to impress the judges—consistently.

THE ROCK OF ANDY MAC

In describing Andy MacDonald and his skating, you only need a single word: consistent. Watch any run in a competition or a clip from a video, and you'll see MacDonald's riding punctuated with a rock-steady commitment to every trick. He has taken the art of contest vert skating and removed all the variables from his runs—before dropping in, he has mapped out everything. He doesn't like to leave anything to chance. His tricks show that.

MacDonald's style comes after years of shaping and refining. While other riders may throw bigger airs,

IN-LINE ± SKATING

The introduction of the modern roller skate to the world was a disaster, but as a public spectacle, it was at least memorable. The year was 1760. Belgian inventor John Joseph Merlin had created the world's first metal-wheeled roller skates, and he was eager to show off his inspired creation. As his showcase, he chose a masquerade ball in London that promised to be crowded with local glitterati.

With the party in full swing, Merlin strapped on his skates, took up his violin, and began to play. Then, to the astonishment of the partygoers, Merlin swooped across the crowded ballroom. Parting like the Red Sea, guests marveled at the mysterious apparition of a violin-playing gentleman swiftly gliding through their midst.

Then they watched in horror as Merlin crashed full tilt into a massive mirror at the far end of the room. Merlin obliterated the mirror and destroyed his violin. In his eagerness, it seems, to unveil his astounding invention, Merlin had neglected to invent brakes.

RECENT RENAISSANCE

The Chicago Skate Company had made and marketed the innovative design of in-line skates in the early 1960s, but they didn't catch on. Fortunately, two hockey-playing brothers, Scott and Brennan Olsen of Minneapolis, Minnesota, were rummaging through a bin containing used sporting goods in 1979, when they found a discarded pair of in-line skates.

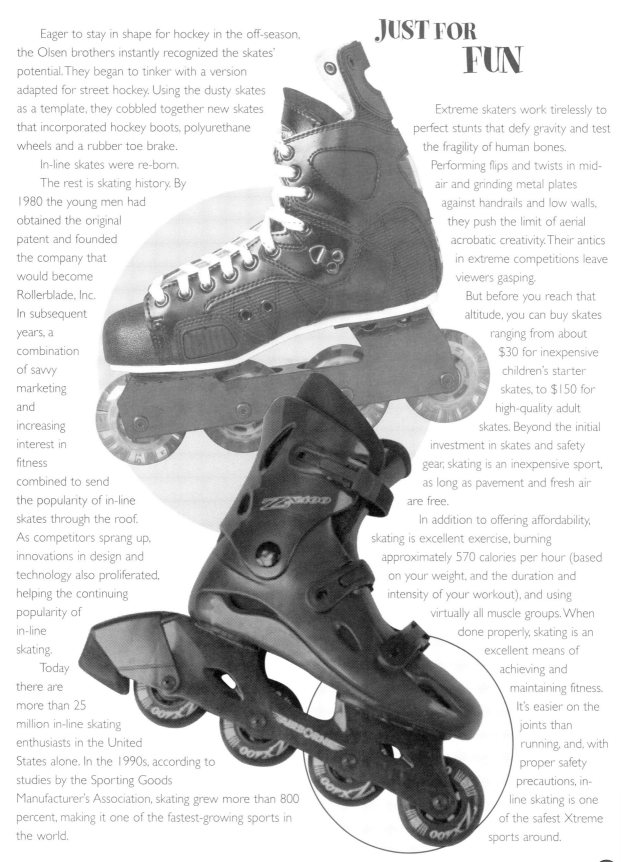

Eager to stay in shape for hockey in the off-season, the Olsen brothers instantly recognized the skates' potential. They began to tinker with a version adapted for street hockey. Using the dusty skates as a template, they cobbled together new skates that incorporated hockey boots, polyurethane wheels and a rubber toe brake.

In-line skates were re-born.

The rest is skating history. By 1980 the young men had obtained the original patent and founded the company that would become Rollerblade, Inc. In subsequent years, a combination of savvy marketing and increasing interest in fitness combined to send the popularity of in-line skates through the roof. As competitors sprang up, innovations in design and technology also proliferated, helping the continuing popularity of in-line skating.

Today there are more than 25 million in-line skating enthusiasts in the United States alone. In the 1990s, according to studies by the Sporting Goods Manufacturer's Association, skating grew more than 800 percent, making it one of the fastest-growing sports in the world.

JUST FOR FUN

Extreme skaters work tirelessly to perfect stunts that defy gravity and test the fragility of human bones. Performing flips and twists in mid-air and grinding metal plates against handrails and low walls, they push the limit of aerial acrobatic creativity. Their antics in extreme competitions leave viewers gasping.

But before you reach that altitude, you can buy skates ranging from about $30 for inexpensive children's starter skates, to $150 for high-quality adult skates. Beyond the initial investment in skates and safety gear, skating is an inexpensive sport, as long as pavement and fresh air are free.

In addition to offering affordability, skating is excellent exercise, burning approximately 570 calories per hour (based on your weight, and the duration and intensity of your workout), and using virtually all muscle groups. When done properly, skating is an excellent means of achieving and maintaining fitness. It's easier on the joints than running, and, with proper safety precautions, in-line skating is one of the safest Xtreme sports around.

GETTING STARTED

Novice skaters should remember that the National Skate Patrol (NSP) recommends the use of kneepads, elbow pads, wrist guards, and a helmet. If you absolutely despise wearing bulky gear, wrist guards and a helmet will probably prevent the vast majority of mishaps from resulting in anything worse than a bruised ego. Forgo them at your own peril, however.

Skates should fit snugly, but should not pinch the toes. Always begin on a smooth, level surface. Attempting to "get your legs" on a slope is asking for trouble. Likewise, rough, cracked or obstacle-strewn pavement is only going to make learning that much harder. Although skates with inflatable wheels (and a premium price tag) are available for off-road use, ordinary recreational skates roll best on paved surfaces.

Get a feel for your skates by walking a little on a lawn. They will undoubtedly seem awkward at first. When you're ready to give it a whirl, move to level pavement. Bending at the knees and keeping your left foot pointed ahead, push off with your right foot, extending it behind with the toes turned out. This should launch you into a gentle glide forward on your left foot. Bringing your right foot back, shift your weight to it as you push off with your left foot. You should be skating.

Much of your initial practice will involve learning to balance comfortably on one foot. With deeper knee bends and more forceful pushes, you should be able to accelerate without too much effort. Like a sprinter launching off the starting block, you can gain momentum by leaning somewhat forward, with knees bent. But *never* lean back. Try to relax and use your upper body naturally. Move your arms back and forth as you stride from one foot to the other, as if you were gently jogging. Your hands should never cross

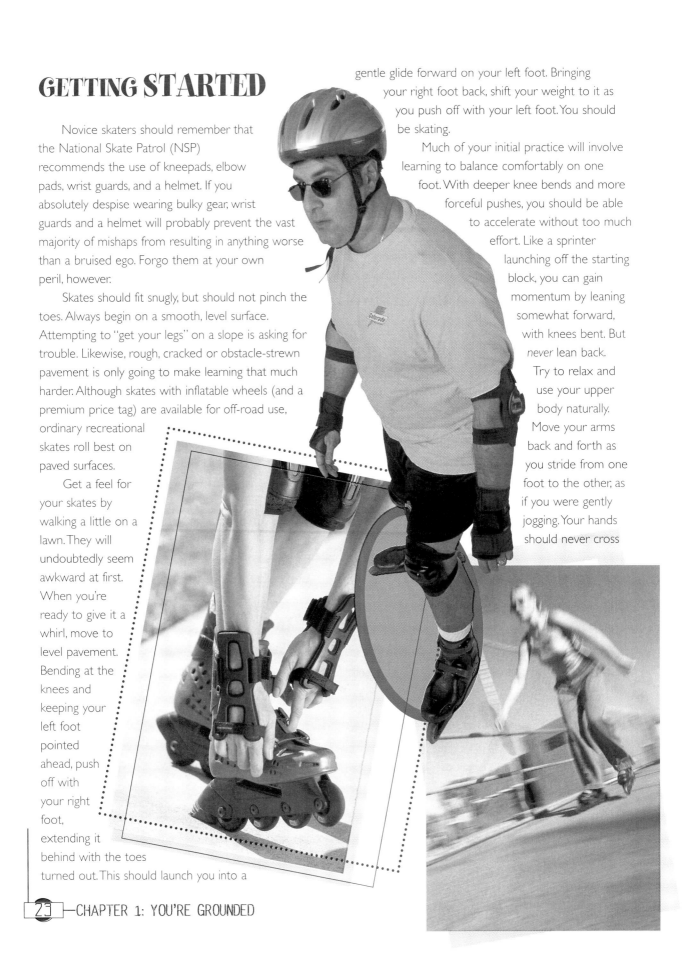

an imaginary line running through the center of your body. Rather, they should stay in alignment with your shoulders. It's possible to roll with both sets of wheels on the ground simultaneously, but economical forward movement depends on a rhythmic pushing off and shifting of your weight from one foot to the other.

HOLD EVERYTHING

Before you go too far, or too fast, it's important to learn how to stop so you do not become the next J.J. Merlin. Your skates will be equipped with some form of rubber, rear-mounted brake pad. Learning to use it effectively takes practice. With most of your weight on the left foot (and the left knee bent slightly), slowly bring your right foot close to your left and raise the toes slightly, while allowing the heel to exert slight pressure on the pavement. Your right heel should be slightly behind your left heel as you carefully exert pressure on the brake.

Continue rolling on your left wheel and support your weight on your left foot as you increase pressure to the right heel and reduce your speed. In this way you should be able to bring yourself to a stop, or to check your speed when it gets out of control on a slope. This all-important maneuver takes practice, but remember taking a spectacular fall is

part of the skating tradition.

Another braking method, borrowed from ice-skating, can be performed with no brake pad at all, but it's not recommended for beginners. Known at the T-stop, it requires you to form a "T" by bringing your angled right foot up behind your forward rolling left foot. The right is dragged, perpendicular to the direction of forward motion, across the pavement behind you. Gradually increasing pressure and adjusting the angle, as needed, a skater is able to come to a complete stop, as the right foot eventually abuts the left foot.

KICKING IT UP A NOTCH

But you want to do all that amazing stuff you see on TV! Well, most of those guys on ESPN have been skating for years, and spend their entire lives doing it, so they have a slight advantage over the weekend park-skater. But here are a few things that can get you on the road to being a fly punk. Good places to practice are parking lots and parking garages that are closed on weekends. Be sure to check with the owner or guard, if there is one, and make sure skating is allowed. Otherwise, an open stretch of pavement or sidewalk just about anywhere will do. Once you have mastered some street skills, you'll be ready to graduate to the skatepark and a half-pipe or pool and learn to do some really insane stuff.

One word of warning, though. Unless you're still 16 and invulnerable, you will want to have kneepads, elbow pads, wrist guards, and a helmet when learning this stuff. Even the pros wear their pads and helmets; they call it ''armor.'' Otherwise, be prepared for a healthy case of road rash. You will fall down. A lot.

On the street, you'll want to learn to do several things. For starters, you need to learn to skate backwards, and more important, to transition from skating forward to skating backwards as a completely natural motion. The easiest way to learn is to get out and do it; surprisingly, your first transition isn't that hard.

While skating forward at a moderate speed, lift one foot an inch or two off the pavement. Then, while leaning forward, swing your weight around. This should make you pivot on the front wheel of the skate that is on the ground. Your momentum will continue to carry you in the direction you were going, but you'll be facing in the opposite direction. To continue moving backwards, you'll simply push against the direction you are going. To return to moving forward (a key to seeing where you are going), simply reverse the action. There is another method, but it requires a lot more coordination and practice. While moving forward, you

essentially hop into the air and make a half twist, landing on the opposite foot from which you started. You should be going backward. You see Olympic ice skaters doing this a lot. There's a reason that they're in the Olympics.

Once you've gotten the hang of basic movement, forward and backwards, try doing some crossovers, that is crossing

your legs over to create a side-stepping motion. As the crossing foot hits the ground, the trailing foot should lift off, otherwise you'll face plant. Learning crossovers is important. It will greatly increase your mobility and your power-generating capabilities, as well as improving your general grace and coordination on skates, which you'll need shortly.

JUMP AND GRIND

Like skateboarders, in-line extremists, or AISs (Aggressive In-line Skaters as they are sometimes referred to), like to slide, grind, and jump on anything that's handy and will support their weight. Unlike a skateboard, which requires a certain finesse to master the most basic move, in-lines are attached to your feet, which means that even a beginner can learn to jump onto a curb or over a big crack in the pavement. All you have to do is jump. As your bravado, balance, and

plate. This is a small section of metal or extremely hard plastic that serves the same function for in-line skaters that trucks and rails do for boarders. They provide a smooth, relatively frictionless surface that can slide perpendicularly across a narrower surface. It is possible to grind without grind plates, but you'll need a slick surface like a pipe-handrail. Otherwise the friction of your wheels sliding sideways will be too much, and you'll face plant. Like most extreme in-line skills, grinding is pretty simple—all you need is a really athletic body and no fear of pain. You can get a lot of advice about finesse, but basically, grinding comes down to jumping onto something and landing on it with the arch of your foot, then sliding along it. Your back foot can be parallel to your front foot, or placed in endless variations, each providing different ratios of control to speed. Other than practice, that's all there is too it.

If you get a little street practice with those skills, the next step to becoming a hot vertical skater is to get to a park and on some ramps or a half-pipe. You may have to share with skateboarders, but a number of parks have in-line ramps and pipes, or beginner areas where you can get started without having to worry about being clobbered by

adrenaline rushes grow, you can put more and more power into those jumps, until you're springing onto or over short walls and handrails.

Once you can get even a little bit of air, you can learn to grind. But before you do, you'll want a pair of skates that are made for it. The skates that the pros use have a plate in the middle of the chassis called a grind

a 90 mph nine-year-old. The skatepark is where you'll learn the really spectacular stuff, like getting inverted and doing alley-oops and brainlesses (a backflip/540 degree turn in the air done on a ramp). But all of the more extreme moves are grounded in the few simple parking lot skills: front and back movement, crossovers, jumps, and grinds.

WHAT ABOUT GEAR?

Most recreational skates feature four wheels with precision bearings designated ABEC 1, 3, 5, or 7, etc. Bearings are by far the most important factor determining the speed, performance, and even price of skates. Fancy brakes and comfortable boots are extras. It's bearings that determine how hard you'll have to work to get things rolling. As a novice, consider purchasing skates with bearings rated ABEC 3 or higher. Unrated bearings are generally not worth the investment, except possibly for young children.

Skates also feature a wide range of wheels, differing in hardness (durometer) and diameter, with the most common sizes ranging from about 72 to 80 millimeters. Occasional skaters who value a smooth ride will probably want to look for low durometer wheels. These absorb shock better, but wear out more quickly than harder durometer wheels. Wheels and bearings are replaceable, and bearings can, and should, be cleaned after many miles of use. Wheels should be checked for wear, and rotated like the tires on an automobile for maximum benefit.

Speed skaters feed the need for speed on five-wheeled skates designed for maximum velocity. They also feature the fastest bearings available, but ordinary recreation or fitness skaters will probably want to stick with four-wheeled skates.

WHERE TO SKATE

For information about the International In-line Skating Association, call (910) 762-7004. Or visit its Web site at www.iisa.org.

Since the demise of the nation's rail system in the 20th century, thousands of railway miles have become available for transformation into trails and greenways. Paved rail-trails cut through cities and run across bucolic rural areas nationwide. They're ideal destinations for skaters, offering long stretches of smooth, relatively level skating surface.

In places like Manhattan's Central Park, skaters fill closed-off streets on weekends, and skating clubs organize weeknight tours of the city and its boroughs in the warm months. In Paris, thousands of skaters take to the city streets every Friday night in a spectacle known as Le Fever. Local authorities cooperate to make the popular weekly event fun and safe. In downtown Indianapolis, skaters cruise the multi-mile Monon rail trail through downtown.

For more information, contact the National Skate Patrol about starting a skating club in your area, or consider joining an existing club, if available. For NSP chapter start-up information, contact Rick Short at (609) 859-5545.

LUGE ON

The art of street luging comes down to navigating a board made of wood or metal while lying flat on your back, with your head just inches from the pavement. Speeds can reach 90 miles per hour. It's a dangerous sport that requires subtle skills and a lot of guts.

A typical race might consist of six racers zooming downhill, bumping and passing their competitors to be the first to the finish line, or it may be a time trial in which a single competitor races alone against the clock. In either case, it's exhilarating to watch, and even more exciting to participate in.

HOW IT WORKS

Street lugers depend on gravity to gain speed and subtle shifts of the body to maintain control. For serious racers, that means each sled must be custom-built. For those who are in it just for fun, buying a ready-made model is fine, but it can be expensive. Finding the right board could mean spending anywhere from $500 to $2,000. (Maybe that's why many opt to build their own by using a plan from the Internet and picking up parts from sporting goods stores or motorcycle shops.)

Most luges are around 6 feet long, 16 inches wide, 14 inches high, and weigh 25 to 30 pounds. To be sure your board fits your body, use this guide: (1) Leg section: Measure from the underside of your feet to your bottom and add eight inches; (2) Torso section: Bottom to mid-neck, plus another eight inches; (3) Head section: Mid-neck to top of head, plus eight inches.

There are several parts that make up a luge:
- Headrest
- Seat
- Handlebars
- Skateboard trucks
- Chassis
- Foot pegs

The finished product will look something like a straightened, streamlined dentist's chair on wheels. In addition to the luge, an athlete will need other paraphernalia. The elite shell out up to $1,500 for a custom-stitched leather race suit, complete with extra padding in the seat, calves, and elbows, plus a

plastic pad to protect the spine. Head protection comes in the form of a full-face motorcycle helmet which has been modified to give the luger a clear line of sight—that's important when reaching speeds close to 100 miles per hour. And finally, protecting the eyes is crucial—that means a face shield or goggles.

For amateurs, gear doesn't need to be so pricey. Here's what you'll need:

- Leather from head to toe
- A motorcycle helmet with a face shield or goggles
- Padding wherever you can put it; the more the better
- Sturdy gloves
- Shoes with thick soles (these will serve as your breaks)

Racing breakneck on a street luge may have you clamoring to know exactly how fast you're going, and without a speedometer the task might seem hopeless. Fear not. Remember all that math your teachers forced you to learn? It's finally going to come in handy.

The only things you need to know to figure out your speed is the distance you traveled and how long it took. Simply divide your distance by your time and then multiply that total by .68 to get your speed in miles per hour.

Here's what the formula looks like:
Rate = Distance/ Time
If your distance is 1,000 feet and your time is 10 seconds…
1,000/10 = 100 feet per second.

To convert it to miles per hour, remember that there are 3,600 seconds in an hour and 5,280 feet in a mile. 3,600 divided by 5,280 is .68. So…100 × .68 = 68 miles per hour

What a rush! Makes you want to go out and get started, doesn't it?

Remember that the first street luges were built out of skateboard parts, and the sport probably has its early origins among skaters who laid down on their skateboards and went screaming down a hill. The equipment has become more specialized, and manufacturers are actually making parts specifically for luges, but the essential elements are still very much like those used in skateboards. The basic element is the truck, a T-shaped piece of metal that connects the axles and wheels to the bottom of the luge. The truck has a flexible interconnection to the bottom of the board, which allows the rider to change the angle on inclination between the bottom of the board and the wheels by leaning. This causes the wheels on the downward side of the board to pull closer together and results in a turn. This is the same way a skateboard is steered, but the trucks on a luge are somewhat wider than those on a skateboard, which makes for greater stability and allows for more flex and greater maneuverability. This is a must due to the high speeds and curved courses lugers must maneuver in competition.

TRICKS OF THE TRADE

Making a name in this very young sport involves competition, but there are tricks that can be used to get a leg up.

First, start with yourself. You will need plenty of upper body strength to start and steer well, so start working out.

Your equipment can make or break you as an athlete. It's true that harder wheels are ideal for speed. They are also more slippery on the road. Also, bearing rating, as with skates, play a role in the top speeds you can reach. It's always a tradeoff between speed and maneuverability. The most important thing is to fine-tune your equipment. Be sure all the parts are correctly aligned and properly functioning in order to maximize your ability for speed. Being comfortable while you ride can help, too, allowing you to focus on maneuvering rather than readjusting.

Once you're at ease with your gear, try learning tactics. Drafting is used in auto racing and has been adopted by street luging. It involves following closely behind your competition, traveling in his wake. The technique is used to keep up speed and save energy in order to win a race at the last moment.

RUBBING IS RACING

Street luge takes a number of cues from auto racing, both in a strategic sense as well as on safety issues. Because of the high speeds involved, the potential for injury is very high, and the rules tend to be fairly stringent about what you can and can't do. There are a number of different governing bodies worldwide for street luge, but the fundamentals are essentially the same among all of them.

While racing, an overtaking rider bears the full responsibility for any collision that occurs. But lead riders may not deliberately swerve into the path of an overtaking rider as a defensive maneuver. The common-sense rule is that riders will have some contact due to the close nature of street luge racing, but virtually any intentional contact is prohibited. Likewise, any interference with another rider by a rider or a member of his crew is grounds for disqualification.

Even if you decide not to compete, street luge is worth a shot. Talk to other enthusiasts and you'll realize it promises quite a rush for the Xtreme athlete. When

you start down that hill, get ready to experience speed like you've never felt before!

GETTING INVOLVED

Street luge is largely a grassroots sport. To get involved, you'll have to be willing to pursue it mostly on your own, as laws governing the sport vary from place to place.

Most cities and towns have speeding regulations and pedestrian laws. You can even get a ticket for blocking traffic, so always be aware. A good rule of thumb: If a police officer asks you to pack your luge and leave, do it!

Many athletes complain that finding a decent practice hill is tough because there are several things that make a good hill good. Low traffic, no side streets, no pavement reflectors, and a smooth surface are the best conditions. Try looking for dead ends. Some even turn to the city dump. Once you find a good spot, keep it to yourself, or you'll soon be competing with other fanatics.

There are not presently any dedicated street luge runs, and even when the X Games holds its competitions, it simply closes off a stretch of road, puts

up some bales of hay in the corners, and lets them fly.

There are few rules that restrict street luge as a leisure activity. You don't have to be licensed or a certain age in order to ride. But if you decide to compete, the lax attitude about the sport changes.

Races take place all over the world from Australia to Europe to North America. For those who fall in love with the sport and wish to do it professionally, options are limited. The best way to make money with street luge is to compete. The cash prizes can be rewarding for winners, but competition is stiff. Athletes who make a name for themselves may take the next step toward endorsements, but that path is reserved for the truly exceptional rider.

THE LAW OF THE LAND

The ultra event for the sport is ESPN's X Games. The extreme athletes who compete in these Olympic-style games vie for more than $400,000 in prize money and qualify through a series of events.

The rules differ at each competition, depending on the governing association, but the organization that calls itself the "premier sanctioning body" of the sport is known as Extreme Downhill International (EDI). Formed in 1995 by Perry and Laurie Fisser, EDI promotes street luge through "safe, fun, fair, and competitive events."

There are other organizations aimed at the same goals, such as the International Gravity Sports Association, the National Street Luge Association, and Racers Association of International Luge, that serve to better the sport with competition and promotion. But it's the enthusiasts who make street luge the phenomenon it is.

PARK IT

Much to the surprise of the wheeled community (and probably the rest of the world), sports such as skateboarding have become popular enough over the last few years to attract more attention from the media and become more accepted as a legitimate sport. Whatever the reason, these sports are bigger and "cooler" than ever, and with this growth comes an increasing number of skateboard parks being built in cities around the world.

Anyone who has tried knows that simply learning to stand on a skateboard is a difficult enough task. Learning a few tricks, or learning to master the art of skateboarding, may take years. But learning the skills and

etiquette to survive and to enjoy a session in a skatepark on a busy day is one of the toughest challenges any skater will ever face. In a crowded skatepark, the most gentle and tolerant individuals can morph into monsters. Some of the top professionals in the world have been known to explode into fits of rage—screaming and destroying their skateboards out of frustration.

Skateparks come in all different forms. They range from huge, public, outdoor, concrete-built facilities to smaller, privately owned, wooden or metal facilities in warehouses to a combination of the two in, of all places, shopping malls.

Most skateparks feature numerous obstacles. They include half-pipes (yeah, those are the big ramps you see on ESPN while channel surfing), mini-half-pipes (a four- or five-foot-high version of a half-pipe), bowls (made to simulate in-ground pools), other ramps of all shapes and sizes, benches, railings, stairs, pyramids, wooden islands and platforms, parking blocks, and almost anything else that the people who designed and built that park could concoct. Some of these parks are free; others charge an admission.

Although originally designed for skateboarding (which makes up the largest percentage of participants), these facilities don't discriminate. Unfortunately, mixing novice (or even intermediate) skateboarders with experts is problematic in itself. Throw BMX bikers, in-line skaters, and those out-of-control scooter riders (of all ages and skill levels) into the mix, and you've got a potentially massive pile-up.

Let's start with the 6-to-11-year-old kids. You were one once. And let's just assume they are novices. (Of course there are always brilliant, prodigy-skater exceptions.) Usually inexperienced, and probably a bit intimidated, these little runts basically use the ramps as they would a slide or a jungle gym in their local picnic and recreation area. Sure, they came in with their skateboards, scooters, and rollerblades—but when these kiddies realize that they are helpless on obstacles that are larger than they are, their accessories are left aside while they play "tag" or some other schoolyard game. To be blunt: These kids get in the way. Why their parents drop them off here is a mystery. Would you bring an 8-year-old to a place made of wood, sheet metal, screws, nails, and concrete? Would you then expect him to survive with other skaters full of energy and experience, twice his age and size, sometimes very

aggressive, and moving at high velocities on skateboards and BMX bikes? It is not uncommon to look out on the skatepark floor and see a group of little ones fleeing for their lives from the path of an irritated skater who is just trying to find a clear runway to a ramp without someone being in the way. The little kids usually just move to another ramp to play.

Then we have the intermediates, usually in their early teens. By this age, the scooters are no longer "cool," and intermediates have denied they ever owned one, but add in the BMX, and you'll wish the scooters were there instead. The problem with the bikes is that they are larger and faster than skateboards, and the person riding them is usually well padded in safety gear. Therefore, he or she is not afraid of anything—at least not as scared as the skateboarder (usually wearing minimal or no safety gear) who may get run over.

A dilemma more obvious than the bike problem is that of the spastic intermediate in-line skaters and skateboarders. To the average observer, this breed may seem to have a handle on the whole Xtreme skating thing. They might look somewhat in control and somewhat capable. Don't be fooled—they aren't any more qualified than you are. In a skatepark, there are dozens of people trying to do their thing on a given obstacle before moving on. The intermediates are known to linger at the bottom of a ramp after they use it, thus blocking the way for anyone else who may come next. What they are doing, we may never know.

Are they waiting for applause? Usually (unbeknownst to them) they are just waiting to get train-wrecked.

Finally, there's the superior group, which usually ranges in age from the late teens to late twenties, and consists mostly of skateboarders and BMXers. An optimal time to witness this elite group at its finest would be on a late weeknight or Sunday night session, while all the kiddies are tucked in bed. On a night like this, there's a kind of harmonic conversion among all those attending the park. There will be euphoria, adrenaline, excitement, and enjoyment—not to mention some insane skating and riding. And accidents are a rarity.

2
ALL THE
ROAD RAGE

Ever since you were a kid, you've loved playing around in the dirt. It only stands to reason that as you've gotten older, you still love it, but you just need better toys. And, of course, now you may be a little more concerned with how cool you look while kicking up dust on the trail or catching big air. After all, there are more people to impress than when you were eight.

Whether you want to crank over a single-track trail, use a motor to push you to the head of the pack, or just hot dog to clamoring crowds, take a look through the next few pages to get a jump on the competition. Anyone from weekend warriors to hammerheads can dig into the information we've compiled about the wide world of dirt. So here's the scoop.

MOTO CROSS

Is it the violent whine of those high pitched engines? Is it the modern-day body armor that makes the riders look like futuristic knights dueling it out? Maybe it's just the unreal big air that riders relish, defying gravity as well as what most anyone would consider sanity. Whatever, people are loving it. Today, motocross racing is large and in charge, and with a newfound TV audience, the sport is making its way into the mainstream at breakneck speed.

What has attracted many to motocross for years is the fun factor for just about anybody. Riders from age four to 60 can race and compete at their own pace; there seems to be a level for just about everyone. This diversity has made motocross one of the most popular forms of amateur motorcycle racing around. What also adds to the fun is that you can race all types of bikes. With racing classes for engines that size anywhere from 50cc to 500cc, it is no problem finding a bike to crank out on most tracks.

STARTING YOUR ENGINE

Okay, you've seen the bikes and the crazy jumps, but you want to know how a punk like yourself can get started. You've got a bike, you ride trails for kicks, and now you think you are ready to battle the tight turns with other like-minded dirt freaks.

Here is the 411: Motocross races are run over closed courses, using natural terrain and some man-made obstacles to test a rider's skill, smarts, and speed. Tracks include hills, jumps, and tight turns. Though you may think fitness is only for those guys in spandex and tank tops, you would be wise to start pumping up and improving your aerobic capacity. One of the most strenuous sports around, motocross is a hellishly rugged test of endurance for both rider and machine. If you and your bike are not in top shape and dialed in, expect to be eating dust, dirt, and maybe even your own teeth.

"I'VE LOST MY MOTO!"

On race day, most events consist of two or more heats, also called motos. They can be either run for a set period of time or a predetermined number of laps. How do you know who wins? Points, man, it's all about points. These are earned in each moto, based on how you finish. The rider with the best total score is the overall winner. So even if you win your first moto, you need to compete in all of them to have a decent result in the general standings. But maybe we need to step back a second and look at the gear you'll need for speed, as well as how you can find a track and get started on your quest for national championships and free swag.

GEAR UP

Doesn't it blow your mind that you can buy a motor bike for a child as young as four years old? (Don't you wish that were the case when you were that age?) Those bikes are in the pee wee race market, but chances are, unless you are a midget, you'll need something with a little more punch. Kids and teens progress onto 60cc, 80cc, and then 125cc motocross bikes, and so you'll ride 125cc, 250cc, or 500cc two-stroke motocross bikes. Some may even want a four-stroke machine, which has steadier power.

The bikes that you would use to race motocross are not your standard road bikes. They have about 18 inches of suspension to handle the intense

jolts from the jumps and bumps. The bikes are made ultra lightweight and with a single shock rear suspension. To ensure sound stopping, disc breaks are standard.

If you are buying a bike for the first time, then visit your local dealer rather than buying from a private bike seller, such as through a classified ad. Try a two-stroke 125cc, or for the brazen, try the 250cc; any bigger and you'll be headed for trouble at high speeds.

Only the pros can notice a real difference in the ultra-high performance of a bike, but everyone can notice a difference in comfort. Make it fit like a sneaker.

Some bikes are narrower, while others seem wider. When seated you should be able to balance yourself with your toes. Flat feet means it's too small. If it is jacked up too high, it will be hard to handle the bike on the trails. The heavier you are, the more power you will need if you want to be competitive in the trails or on the track. But there's a tradeoff. The bigger the bike, the more it weighs, and the harder it is to handle. Bikes that weigh less will handle better on jumps; on the other hand, a heavier bike can grip the dirt with more authority.

WHAT DO YOU WANT?

With any piece of equipment you plan on buying, you must first figure out what it is you want to do with it. Do you plan on riding trails, motocross, enduros, or trials? The bikes that say they "can do it all" usually can, but they do it all on an average level, at best. Every bike is designed with a particular purpose. Unless your aim is to struggle with your bike up hills because it weighs too much, buying the right bike for the right situation is the only way to go.

STROKING IT

So you want some power, and your buds tell you the four-stroke is for real riders. Two-strokes, they say, are for kids. Don't fall for the machismo stuff; there are reasons to want both, with little of it having to do with macho delusions. In general, a four-stroke engine is better for the trails and enduro races. It will have an easier flow of power, will produce less noise, and require less maintenance. So why a two-stroke? The engine will rev faster, have intense power, and hair-trigger throttle response. It is obvious that most people will want the two-stroke for racing motocross.

LET'S GET SERIOUS

What is the number one priority when riding? That's right, your safety. When racing motocross, not only is it essential that you wear the right safety gear, it's the rule. Here are some riding tips to keep you safe, not sorry.

WHEN YOU NEED TO BAIL

At some point you will stack. When it happens get away from the bike. Don't try to cushion the bike's fall with your body. It doesn't care about you or your well being. Just get away from it.

OUCH, MY BIKE!

You wreck. You come out unscathed but you fear your bike might not have fared as well. Don't panic. Here is some basic bike CPR. First, turn it off, or you'll flood the engine, and starting it again will be a royal pain. Your clutch and brake levers are likely to have taken a beating, so carry spares. One way you can prevent breakage is by changing the position of the levers so that they don't stick out farther than the handlebars. You'll be happy that you did.

Tool kit: Don't leave home without it. Carry all the tools that are needed for routine maintenance and repairs on your bike: spoke wrench, axle wrenches, tire irons, patch kit, air pump, spark plugs, maybe even a spare tube. Things you'll need to check before you go are your chain slack and the level of your bike's fluids. Don't be the fool who seizes an engine because you were too busy adjusting your BJ2 ballistic jersey rather than checking the oil.

Here are some other tips to keep your motor running after a crash. Adjust the perch bolts so they are a little loose. This will allow the brake levers to move on the bars instead of breaking. If they move while you ride then you'll endo. Footpegs and pedals can get mangled, so carrying a spare is wise. Also, if you bust a shift lever, a vice grip can double in an emergency. Finally, stickers are great for protecting the side panels and gas tanks.

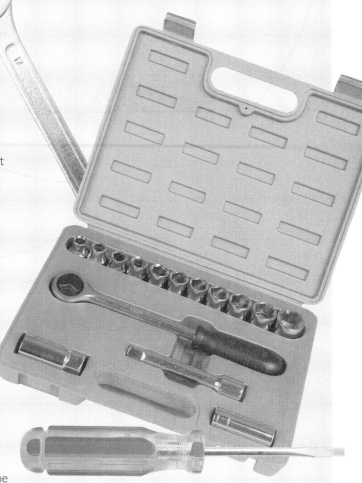

ARMOR IT ALL

Before you race or ride, you'll need to get the gear to keep you out of the hospital. Check with the group that governs your racecourse, for it may have specific standards, especially for the all-important helmet. Never, ever buy one that is used! Helmets are designed to break internally on impact so your head doesn't. A second-hand helmet is simply a risk. Goggles are next. Make sure they fit snugly but not too tight. Your gloves should have plenty of protection over the fingers and knuckles but also be flexible. Body armor is the real cool stuff. Giving you protection for your chest and back, it is essential to wear.

Your race duds are crucial. Aesthetics are everything, as you well know, and your clothes are what turns heads. However, before you pose for the cameras make sure you are wearing knee and elbow pads, as well as a kidney belt underneath it all. Protect your shins and ankles with riding boots. Though they may be uncomfortable at first, they keep you gripped to your bike. In fact all of this stuff takes some time to get used to, so be patient.

DUDE, DO YOU RACE THAT THING?

There are a few more things before the start goes off. You'll need a license to race. The American Motorcyclist Association (AMA) has a huge amateur competition program and can give you more details. Since 1924, it has been organizing events and helping people get started in racing motorcycles. It can help you find a track and even recommend ways to get instruction.

So you think you're ready, but remember, you are not Hurricane Bob Hannah, yet. This is a *very* competitive sport.

THE
RACE

Here is the skinny: There are up to 45 riders on a long, single start line. Their first goal? They all have eyes on the first corner known as the "hole shot." Get there late, and it could be a short race. Because the beginner levels, such as schoolboy classes, are sometimes only 10 minutes long, there is no time to get past all the riders who beat you to the turn. At the higher levels, the races are longer, up to 40 minutes, which gives you more leeway off a bad start. In any case, getting to the hole first will give you a huge advantage.

Most tracks have plenty of jumps and bumps and are made of natural terrain—otherwise known as dirt. Though there can be obstacles that are man-made in the form of tabletops and double jumps, most beginner circuits are not as daunting as those seen in the magazines. Just make sure you practice acceleration, turning corners, and landing off jumps. More important, know your bike and your riding ability inside and out.

FINDing ENLIGHTENMENT

So this seems like a big commitment, and you are not sure about the money and whether you'll even like it. Nice excuse, but there is an answer. Go to a motocross coaching and tryout, where you can even rent the bike and gear for the day. These are usually held at practice times at a local track.

Oh, you have the bike already. You, friend, should still go to a practice track before you sign up for a race. Many pros spend hours working out moves on the practice dirt before they hit the kind that pays. Your local shop will also have ideas on coaches, track practice, and places for you to receive instruction.

There are also loads of camps and schools. The curriculum usually includes safety, cornering, starts (getting to the hole shot!), using the clutch and throttle, jumping, braking, bike maintenance, and race prep. Some well-known schools are the Donnie Hansen Motocross Academy in Colorado and The Fastline Racing School of Southern California. For women there is the Debbie Matthews Women's School of Motocross that travels the country giving instruction.

"BUT I WANT TO BE LIKE RICKY!"

Do you really think Ricky Carmichael started off doing those big moves? No, no one does. What he and other pros participate in is an advanced development of motocross called Supercross. Invented in the U.S., the races take place in stadiums and are incredible to watch. The tracks are full of formidable obstacles, such as tabletops and death defying double and triple jumps.

The racers achieve enormous airtime and do unbelievable tricks, which make for spectacular viewing. Riding and racing at this level are strictly for the experts and professionals.

Since we are on to the pros, here are some who have made the sport of motocross what it is today.

In the late '70s Bob Hannah stole most shows, until a water skiing accident in 1979 knocked him out. Taking over where Bob left off was Rick "Bad Boy" Johnson. Riding for Honda, he too was struck down with a freak injury, his taking place when a rider landed on him during a practice run.

Today it is clear that two riders are dominating most racing: Jeremy McGrath and Ricky Carmichael. The two together have more wins than they know how to count. RC has an amazing 52 percent pro win ratio (he won 55 out of his 106 pro races), and Jeremy has 102 pro wins himself. These super studs are the reigning kings of Supercross, but remember, they, too, had to go through the countless heats on the motocross scene to get to where they are today.

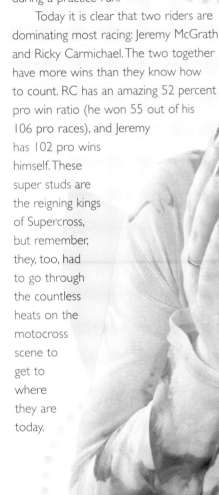

FREESTYLE
MOTOCROSS

Backflips? No way. On a motorcycle? Get outta here. Ask your buddy if anyone can do a backflip on a motorcycle. Then when he says no, point to the 2000 Gravity Games where Carey Hart pulled off the unimaginable. Then tell him you intend to do the same. The key word here is "intend." That backflip was a defining moment for the spanking new sport of freestyle motocross. Still a baby, the sport is smacking the cheese out of other Xtreme events with its high-flying jumps and back-bending tricks. What is it that makes it so much more amazing to watch freestyle motocross than snowboard half-pipe competitions or downhill mountain biking? It must be the bikes. Ask Mr. Evel Knievel. He started this mess, leaping over cars and canyons. Freestyle motocross is just a natural progression in the ongoing saga of humans, airborne motorcycles, and serious injury.

FREE BIRD

So what exactly is freestyle? The expression comes from BMX events in which riders hang in the air, run on set courses, and fly over obstacles. Instead of bicycles, these riders are on motocross bikes. They have a certain amount of time to hit jumps and perform an assortment of moves to be scored by a panel of judges.

With motocross, however, the height and the length of the jumps are so extreme that even a casual viewer can see how crazy and risky they actually are. Basically, the faster you ride, the higher you can fly.

YOUR TURN

So you want to pull supermans and sterilizers, do ya? Yes, you are the guy at the track who is always goofing off, hammering jumps, and pulling off tabletops instead of concentrating on the finish line. You think for a second, "Hey, why not just jump and be merry?" Sounds good to us, but before you start your engine, take a look at who the standouts are. You'll notice that the same names keep popping up at all competitions. This is because not too many riders can do what they do. The stuff you see on TV and in videos takes incredible skill and an ability to block out all fear. Quite frankly, it is extremely dangerous. That's part of freestyle motocross' appeal, but before you start out in the sport, make sure you are ready.

TAKE OFF

First, you'll need a super strong bike. Most freestyle rigs are very similar to motocross track bikes. The differences are in the suspension and frame strength. Bikes come in all sizes, as well as two-stroke and four-stoke models. Some big manufacturers are Honda, Suzuki, and Kawasaki. Find a bike that you like and that fits you like a glove. A bike that is too big will be a nightmare to handle in the air. Proper fit is probably the biggest thing to remember when buying a new bike. You might want to throw on a skid plate, frame guard, and a chain guide for protection.

Assuming you know your bike and have one that can take a beating, what else do you need? First, you need a very good helmet. Shoei and Arai make great lids that also look dope. Pants and jerseys can be had at relatively cheap prices these days and will make you more comfortable on the bike and in the air as well. Underneath it all wear a kidney belt, body armor, and elbow and knee pads. Boots will help place your feet more securely on the pegs when coming back down to earth. Now that you are dressed for success, it is time to face your destiny.

WELCOME TO HARD TIMES

When you roll onto the freestyle track you will be in awe. Once you stare down an enormous gap-jump that leads to a ramp-to-ramp transition, you'll see why. The track is an all-dirt loop, 200 feet by 200 feet, where the riders choose their own fate. The runs usually include monster jumps, scary spines, and diamond hits that would make test pilot Chuck Yeager wet his pants. Once a rider finishes a performance, he is scored on style, difficulty, and originality by a panel of judges.

HUGE AIR

At the core of the freestyle concept are the tricks. To date, the top was Carey Hart's surreal backflip. Throughout Xtreme sports, this created the biggest buzz. TV sponsors came in droves, throwing cash at riders. This is what the people want to see and will pay for.

In the meantime, here is the lowdown on some moves to help jumpstart your pursuit of glory. It will take incredible amounts of time practicing any of these tricks if you want to do them well. Safety is critical, so always ride within your ability. Okay, enough already, it's airtime.

THE TRICKS OF THE TRADE

Physically, you will need to be in top shape. Through riding and working out in the weight room, a rider can prepare for the rigors of the freestyle course. Though being in good aerobic shape is not as necessary as brute strength, increasing lung capacity can help. Why? Because one of the biggest problems many riders face in motocross is "arm pump." Basically, it is when a rider's arms no longer can grip the handlebars. Your arms get extremely hard, and your legendary vice-like grip becomes more like Jell-O. If you ever see someone's riding style change drastically during an event, he may be pumped out. Rock climbers get the same thing on tough climbing routes. How do you fix it? Correct breathing. Opening up your lungs to let the air move the blood to your hands can alleviate the problem. Strong breathing comes only from being in shape. Maybe that is why Travis Pasrana, one of the top riders in the world, doesn't drink or smoke and makes sure his body is running as smooth as his bike.

When you are fit and geared, it is time to learn the moves. The place to go is the track where other riders will be doing the same thing—over, and over, and over again. Practice and patience are the secret to putting the following moves into your riding resume.

First up is the bar hop. This one on a difficulty scale is maybe a seven out of 10. Once in the air, kick both feet straight out between your arms. You need to be in the air long enough to safely get those toes back on the pegs, so don't skimp on speed when approaching the jump. The farther you get your feet over the front fender, the more points you'll score.

Next is the catnac. It is like a can can, in which you move both legs to one side of the bike. This trick takes it a step further by putting your whole body over there. Get out and back before impact, and the crowd will erupt.

Okay, let's turn it up a bit. The sterilizer will do. Sounds nasty doesn't it? Check this out: Put your legs over the handlebars, soar through the air, and leave them there for the landing. Hence the name, and if you miss the landing, hence the pain.

The trick that might get the most press is the outrageous move known as the superman. To do this you must be experienced. First get big, big air. Once aloft, hang onto the bars and let your legs go out behind you. Stay straight and as vertical as possible. Until you need to come back to earth, that is. A nine on the scale of ten.

Time to take it off the charts, eh? The Hart Attack, otherwise known as the superman seat grab is the move of moves. Carey Hart, the man who pulled off the backflip last year, is the inventor of this one as well. How do you do this lunacy? It's the same as the superman, but you grab the seat; yes, the handlebars have to take care of themselves. Go out and ride for a while, say ten years, and then come back and try it. This one needs some time, trust us.

WHERE THE WILD THINGS RIDE

To get to the level of these guys will take time. It is also a good idea to get some instruction. First stop should be the International Freestyle Motocross Association (IFMA). It is one of the governing bodies of this new sport, and can point you in the right direction for track locations and where to learn the tricks from the pros.

Let's face it, the top riders all come from a racing background. Many riders not only raced motocross, but also competed at a very high level before making the transition to freestyle. Many freestyle tricks and techniques were born at the back of the race track, from guys who felt they were out of the money for a top finish and wanted to leave their mark on the crowds with eye popping moves over the big jumps.

Get to the track and race your bike before you start to hit big doubles and pull off catnacs. Watch other guys and what they do and you will learn. Supercross, motocross, heck even trials riding will give you the tools needed to shred the air in a way you never thought possible. Just remember to come back down in one piece. And always wear your helmet.

THE X MEN

Contributing to the overwhelming success of freestyle motocross are the athletes themselves. People say Supercross riders are like this, and freestyle motocross riders are like that. These are just stereotypes, folks. In freestyle, anything goes.

Check out Travis Pastrana. The squeaky clean 17-year-old is all about fun and, darn it, he doesn't even cuss! But he does ride. He is the rookie 125 Outdoor National Champion, and he made some major noise at the Gravity Games. Look for him to be around for many years to come.

Then there is Brian Deegan. Covered in tats and coated in armor that makes him look like he is the post-apocalyptic Mad Max, he is all about being over the top and in your face. Man, he is more like down your throat. MTV has embraced him, as have thousands of fans.

Two other mega-stars are Carey Hart and Mike Metzger. Hart's backflip and Hart Attack have taken this sport to higher ground. Metzger was one of the first to realize that the motor separates this sport from the other Xtreme events. He is the undisputed king of the early videos and is credited with inventing many of the tricks you will no doubt see, as well as attempt.

BMX

new subculture all its own.

In fact, so many people were pumped to ride and do their own thing that BMX splintered into factions. Some folks got into dirt jumping, others got into track, freestyle, and street.

GETTING THE GEAR

KID STUFF

In the 1970s, there was a shift, inspired by planet alignment or some other force, that changed the way a bicycle was to be ridden forever. It first struck a bunch of kids in California when they modified their 20-inch bikes to rock out like their heroes did on the motocross scene.

So these kids, and understand they were kids, raced these bikes on tracks, pulled off tricks in parking lots, and launched themselves on homemade dirt jumps. The result? Bicycle motocross, more commonly known as BMX, became an instant sensation from coast to coast. Innovations multiplied, and soon there was a new sport with new tricks and a

By now you have made the choice to dip into dangerous turns and launch over bumps. But before you hit the track, you need to focus on your bike, protective gear, technique, and timing. With these things dialed, perhaps you will be the new dean of the dirt—if not, the dunce of the day. It is all about the bike, right? Standard BMX-style bicycles have 20-inch wheels and are commonly used on a track. If you want a bigger bike for some reason, BMX bicycles with 24-inch or greater diameter wheels, commonly called cruisers, can be raced, but only at specific events. Some of the dopest rides are made by Haro, Redline, and Nirve, as well as major bicycle manufacturers such as Specialized and GT. Commonly made of aluminum and steel, most bikes can be had for a couple hundred bucks and will suit the novice just fine.

You'll also need to protect yourself before you wreck. And if you plan on racing you'll need to get the protective goods because it's the rule. The referee at any event may disqualify a rider from participation in a race if he determines that the rider's bicycle or protective gear is inadequate. Therefore, a helmet manufactured to meet recognized bicycle safety standards must cover at least halfway down a rider's ears, and it must have a chinstrap. If your helmet is open faced, you'll need to pick up a mouth guard. A long-sleeved shirt and long pants must be worn, as well as shoes with soles soft enough to grip a BMX-style pedal. It will be helpful to wear some knee and elbow pads, and gloves, too. Now that you look like a pro, or at least something out of *Road Warrior*, it is time to ride.

WHERE TO GET YOUR GROOVE ON

It is easy to start racing BMX. Once you throw down for the bike and the clothes, you need to find a track. The races will likely be sanctioned by one of the two BMX governing bodies: The for-profit American Bicycle Association (ABA) or the non-profit National Bicycle League (NBL). The NBL is the only sanctioning body in the U.S.A. recognized by Union Cycliste Internationale (UCI), the international governing body of all bicycle racing. These two organizations are the places to go for information on track locations, rules, racing licenses, and race points. It can be worth your while to contact them before you spend any loot on stuff you might not need, like oversized axles or jumping wheels.

Once you find a track, line up a race date and commit to it. It only costs a few dollars to enter a series of weekend races. Spring for a one-day temporary license until you know this BMX nonsense is for you. That's it: You look the part, you are legal and registered, and you are good to go.

BURN FAT to GET PHATTER

Though BMX racers aren't pushing the envelope of exercise boundaries or engaged in groundbreaking training regimens, they do have to be fit. So how do you get ready to race? Most pros spend a good deal of time on trails as well as on the track. Riding singletrack, similar to the trails mountain bikers frequent, will teach you the skills. Because a BMX bike doesn't have any gears, the trails need to be flat and rolling in order to keep you moving. The other way to build leg strength is to hit the weights. The pros do endless squats, keeping the weight relatively high and reps low—remember this isn't the Tour de France here, you need to be fast only for a minute. Healthy food and plenty of liquids of the non-alcoholic variety will do you well, too. If this doesn't cut the mustard, word has it that a healthy dose of Girl Scout cookies, preferably those Peanut Butter Patties, will greatly enhance race day performance.

IN YOUR FACE RACE

The great thing is, no matter how dope you think you are, the NBL and the ABA say you will have to start at the bottom. There are four generally recognized proficiency levels in the guy's 20-inch classes: rookie, novice, expert, and AA pro. Want to turn pro? Don't count your bucks yet; you'll need to move up classes with wins and top placements. Win a race, you will get points. The more points you get, the quicker you move up. Every race starts with motos, which are three qualifying rounds. Each group of riders, with a maximum of eight riders per group, races each other three times. The best four from each heat over those three initial rounds transfer to the next round of racing. Sometimes there are variations on the size of the group and number of heats, but regardless, be prepared to go the distance a number of times throughout the day.

What you need to know to excel in BMX racing is that it takes quickness and power, as well as bike handling and a tactical strategy. Many consider it the most technical form of bicycle racing. Why? Depending on the length and technical difficulty of the track, a BMX race usually lasts a whopping 30 to 40 seconds. The track itself is only 300 to 400 meters long, so putting in long training miles is about as helpful as wearing a new pair of underpants. You want to be explosive, like a linebacker on steroids. Erupting off the start and being able to withstand the bumping that takes place on the track is your key to finishing ahead of the pack.

FRESH OUT OF THE BOX

More so than any other form of bike racing, in BMX, the start is everything. When you are at the gate, have one foot on the ground and the other one on the pedal. The pedal should be at its highest point in order to hammer the cranks down as soon as the gate drops. Wrong pedal placement and it's over before you even hit the dirt. Your front wheel will be against a metal gate, which will drop at the start. Push with your upper body to thrust your bars down onto the track. Good follow-through pedal strokes get you out front. Practice timing your hip movement and pedal power until you

get a snap without pushing the gate, which can slow you down. Things to remember: Timing, snap your hips, follow-through strokes, win.

Though you may have seen the pictures in the mags of guys pulling off barspins and tailwhips, that stuff won't help you here. Why? You can only accelerate when your wheels are on the ground. A general rule of thumb is to keep them rolling, not airborne. Stay low on the jumps and keep the air minimal. The method? By letting the front wheel get some loft and crouching over the first peak, you can force the front wheel to stay elevated when the rear wheel starts down the back of the first peak. You will be in a wheelie, otherwise known as a manual, from the back of the first jump to the second jump. When the front wheel clears the second peak, you can drop the front end down the second backside and crouch as you go over. This keeps the bike from lifting off the jump and allows you to straighten your legs and begin pedaling, which is what gives you that all-important thrust. The tracks are designed to send the neophytes flying, so watch the experts and pros. Off the seat, they try to keep the pedals turning and the bike moving. Unless you're some pro-animal who can flip doubles and still place top three, stay on the down low and keep it real.

At the finish, keep hammering. Too many racers let up down the stretch, where placement between the first five riders can be nanoseconds. These races are short and fast, so don't let up until you cross the line. If you stay focused and work hard, the wins will come, and before you know it, GT will be calling you out to Huntington Beach to do TV promos for Mountain Dew. Doesn't hurt to dream.

WHO IS RAD?

You are dude! But there are others. Some of the biggest names hark back to the days when *Three's Company* ruled TV, and many a good man wore a mullet and a mustache because he thought it would land him chicks in cut-off denim shorts and sporting feathered hair. One of those guys was Stu Thompson, ABA's very first No.1 Pro in 1979 and who rode for Huffy in the mid-'80s. Known as Stompin' Stu, he is perhaps the biggest name BMX has. Another legend is Greg Hill, who in 1977 turned pro at the age of 13 and hasn't stopped since. He has raced for Redline, Mongoose, and GT during his long career, and like many racers who want to dabble on the production side, even started his own companies —GHP, Greg Hill Speed Seminars, and Dope BMX Products. As for the dames, Cheri Elliott might be top diva of all time. With three consecutive ABA No.1 titles ('83, '84, '85), Cheri is arguably the girl with the most cake, or at least wins. So fast in her prime, she often beat the boys. Where is she now? Stomping and romping as usual, just now on downhill and dual slalom mountain bikes, on the NORBA (National Off Road Bicycle Association) circuit.

As for the new school, there is so much talent around the globe it is scary. Christopher Leveque, riding for Specialized, is a French phenom who won everything there was in Europe, so he moved to California in 1994 in search of some competition. The Flyin' Frenchman has been credited with taking the AA pro class to a whole new level.

Danny Nelson is another top dog on the pro circuit. Factory-sponsored since the age of six, "Thunder" has been close to ranking No. 1 for the past few years.

Two of the hottest rising stars in BMX are actually not from California. Matt "Rickus" Pohlkamp lives in Ohio, and has mad skills from years of riding trails and

tracks. Another one to watch is Jamie Staff (a Brit) with Haro-Adidas. As one pro has said, "The dude's got some frogs!" Translation: He has beefy legs that know how to pound the pedals. It's the power of those pistons that has given Haro's British bomber plenty of wins and year-end rankings in the Top 10.

KICKING THE NEW KNOWLEDGE

Though most street riders will call you a chump if you admit to seeking organized instruction, it can be a great way to get fast faster. BMX racing camps are springing up all over the country and offer every level of training. The pro Mat Hoffman and companies like GT run summer camps. Many have scholarships for those dying to learn how to ride better but who don't have the money. Another way to learn is just going to the local track and watching the more experienced riders. This helps as does talking to those who work at the local track or shop. But let's face it, nothing is better than experience. Turn off your PlayStations. Download the new Slipknot some other time. This stuff won't make you fast. Go ride and race. That will.

FREESTYLE BMX

are dedicated to just one. Geography plays a part too. For example, street riders are mostly located in the cities, while dirt jumpers may come from areas with more open space. Before we get to the tricks, we'll define what each style is in a little more detail.

Nac-nacs and tailwhips. A no-footed nose pick. Superman seat grabs. No, these aren't the newest pro wrestling moves. These are for real, and they are tricks of the BMX trade, which has vaulted into one of the most popular Xtreme sports in the world. What started in the '70s as a way for California kids to look and act like their motocross heroes has now been taken to another level, with riders rocking out signature moves everywhere from the urban skate parks in the East to hill jumps in the Midwest.

Freestyle BMX has opened up the world of 20-inch bikes to thousands. How did it happen? The freedom and creativity involved in freestyle are the major factors. No longer are bike riders stuck to the races on dirt and the track. Whether you live in the Bronx or Beijing, chances are you can find a place to ride freestyle in some way, shape, or form.

And the variations in this sport are growing. Just as BMX has two distinct categories—racing and freestyle—freestyle itself can be broken down into further subsets. There are four major groups of riding: Street, vert, dirt jumping, and flatland. Some BMXers ride in all styles and also race, but others

STREET

Street is usually just heading to town and hitting everything possible—with the bike, not your body of course. It's open season on handrails, benches, curbs, drop-offs, steps, and walls unless the cops say otherwise. Beware, because hardcore street riding can be dangerous. If you enter a street competition, expect a variety of ramps, rails, and other urban obstacles that are made of metal and concrete.

FLATLAND

In terms of technical difficulty, flatland tricks may be the hardest to pull off because there are fewer hills. Riders won't improve unless they practice. You'll need excellent timing and great equilibrium, even though most of the tricks are on the pavement, not in the air. Many of the flatland bikes are shorter than traditional BMX bikes and weigh less, giving you a little edge in terms of tricks.

VERT

This style of riding is what attracts all the publicity these days, and for good reason: It is simply amazing to watch. It is by far one of the most hardcore and extreme types of freestyle riding, and just learning to ride in the half-pipe takes serious cajones. Riders can reach heights over 12 feet, nail spinning 360s, and do backflips. This sport is not for the faint of heart—and maybe just for the insane.

DIRT JUMPING

Why dirt jump? Because that's what the motocross guys were doing and that's the reason many kids started racing in the first place. Speed and big air mean dope tricks and make this BMX style the most popular with both riders and spectators.

EXPRESSING YOURSELF

So you consider yourself an artist, but you don't paint. You are looking for a way to show the world your vibrant and strong life force, that personal power and creative flow, but you just can't seem to find an outlet. Freestyle BMX might be the answer, and though most anyone can get into this game, there are a few prerequisites.

The two most important things you'll need are patience and bravery. No rad freestyler is afraid to fall or fail. You will do both hundreds if not thousands of times. When you are ready to commit to being disciplined, go get a 20-inch bike, rig it out with a grind disc or a sprocket guard, wear some cool baggy threads and a jumping helmet, and you'll be ready to roll. Well, sort of.

NO GUTS, NO GLORY

Overcoming fear is the bottom line. If you roll up a vert ramp and flake out while trying a bar spin, you'll pay. Big time. You must face fear head on, and understand there is a learning curve here. You will bail—often. Make that very often. Wear protective gear: helmet, knee, and elbow pads, shin guards, a mouth guard, even body armor if need be. This stuff will give you peace of mind. Everyone, pros included, endures countless crashes and injuries for the sake of catching big air this way.

Equally important is being patient. This stuff is hard, seriously. As with skateboarding, you will have to practice all the time and be willing to make it a lifestyle if you want to hit the pipe or win competitions. Set your goals first. Ask yourself, "Do I want to win vert events with 360-tailwhips or just cruise and grind curbs on flatland?" Understanding where you want to take yourself on your bike will dictate the time, money, and effort you put in.

Like most, you probably have seen the X Games on TV or a video in which dudes launch off crazy drop-offs and contort and twist in ways never thought possible. You may even dream of being the next Mat Hoffman or Dave Mirra. The announcers scream your name. The girls throw themselves at you and the corporate sponsors toss money—wake up! You have some things to learn first, like the tricks.

HOW TO BUST A MOVE

So many moves, so little talent. There are many tricks to be tried and all kinds of variations. Here are a few basic tricks in each style as well as the how-to on a few only the bold would dare to attempt. As with most tricks, start out small and gradually go bigger each time you try one.

THE BASICS: DIRT JUMPING

Dead Sailor

When you are airborne, stiffen your arms and legs. That's it, Evel Knievel. This is the easiest of the bunch.

Bar-Turn

Turn your bars to the left or the right. Turning your bars and twisting your head and upper body the full 90 degrees gets you extra style points. And style is everything—hence the "style" in freestyle.

Kickout

As soon as your back wheel leaves the jump, swing the rear of your bike around to the right or the left by using your hips and legs. But don't stay sideways very long. Land crooked, and you'll bail. Gradually swing the rear of your bike out farther each time you jump, and you'll eventually reach a full swing of about 80 degrees.

One-Footer

Simply take your foot off your pedal, kick it out to the side, and stick it back on before you land. Your cranks will rotate downward when your foot comes off, so get it back on in time to return your cranks to a level position.

One-Hander

This is pretty simple too, and is sometimes easier to learn by pulling up hard on your bars. Once the bike is almost vertical, take a hand off the grip. Just a little at first and try to keep your bars straight the whole time. Simple right?

Can-Can

Same as a one-footer except you take your leg across the top tube of your bike. Take your left leg and stretch it way out over your top tube to the right of your bike. That's it. Then bring that leg back over the bar before you land or your hips will be permanently planted deep into your chest cavity.

Cross-Up (X-Up)

A dope trick, but make sure you can spin your handlebars all the way around without the seat getting in the way. Lean back and spread your legs apart in the air to give room for the handlebars to spin. Turn your bars a full 180 degrees left or right. Then whip them back the other way. Don't get discouraged if you can't get a full 180 rotation at first. Remember, it's all about practice.

Tabletop

You may have heard about this one. A staple move of many a rider, it can be done in either direction. Push down on your handlebars to the right and turn them down to the left at the same time, while using your right leg and lower body to push the rear of your bike up and to the left into a horizontal position. Gradually level your bike out more and more each jump, until you reach a perfectly flat position. Get it? Flat, table, tabletop?

360

Steppin' it up are you? Believe it or not, you don't really need a lot of air to do a 360 (a full rotation on the bike). But it may be wise to practice on flat ground first. Simply try to do a bunnyhop 360. You might not pull it off at first, but try to at least do a 180. As on a snowboard, start spinning before you leave the ground. Turn your head and handlebars hard to the left or right, whichever you prefer, and rotate with everything you've got. Your body follows your head as you spin. Don't go too fast at first. Going slow, you can usually get away with an under-rotation, but with more speed—oh the pain!

MOVES FOR STREET/VERT

Wheelie & Manual

Just as you did it as a kid, pull the bars up and pedal. That's it. However, in a manual you don't pedal. You just pull back on the bars, lean back, and use your legs, not the pedals, to keep you going. Lean way back by your rear wheel with your arms relaxed. When you feel the front end dropping, flex your arms and knees in and out, which will keep the front end up. Confused? It is actually easier done than said.

Nosepick

First bunnyhop, hit your front brakes, then push the front end of the bike down into an endo (in which your rear wheel goes airborne). Aim for the edge of whatever you are trying to nose-pick—curb, wall, whatever—and balance there on your front wheel with your front brakes firmly locked. After a second or two, do a hop on a little front wheel just before jumping back off. This trick is used often in street and ramps, so it is worth it to learn the move well.

Feeble grind

No, you yourself are not the feeble grind, though you might feel like one. It is a move in which your rear peg, those metal cylinders on the wheel's hubs, grinds across a surface. Ride up to the wall slowly and bunnyhop up with your rear peg grinding across the wall and your front wheel rolling across it. Before you come to a stop, bunnyhop up and off the wall. Try it first on a wall or something that slopes down and use wax on the wall to smooth out the grind.

FLY ON FLATLAND

Tailwhip

This trick looks really cool. Take your right foot across the top tube, over to the left side of your bike, and place it on the front tire. Swing the rear of the bike around using your right foot and take your left foot off the pedal (simultaneously). Keep your left foot up high, aim it at the top tube, and use it to catch the rear end of the bike when it whips around. When the rear of the bike swings back around, plant your left foot on the top tube. With your left foot still on the top tube, take your right foot off the tire and put it back on the right pedal. Balance, put the left foot on the pedal next, balance, and ride. Rad move.

Infinity Rolls

To do this, put one foot on a back peg and push off backward with the other foot and use that foot to scuff, or roll, the tire backwards in a circle. Your peg foot should be on the outside of the circle. With your handlebars turned at 45 degrees you can roll forever, hence infinity rolls. Make sure you have a finger on the break to keep you steady.

Rockwalk

Roll into a small arc, squeeze your front brakes, and lift the back of your bike up to about 180 degrees and turn a half rotation. After the back wheel comes down to the pavement, spin another 180 degrees on the back wheel. The key is keeping the drive and movement going through the stop and starts.

BE LIKE A PRO

You're saying to yourself, "Man, those moves are weak sauce. I need to break off the two comma type jams so a major factory sets me up. Damn!" (Translation: I need to be able to do the $1,000,000 moves to get some sponsorship money.) Well, here is a taste of what you'll need to know. Remember, these tricks are no joke. The real way to wow the crowds and bring the noise is to invent your own moves, and link those and other tricks in a unique way.

Flare

A flare is basically a backflip with a 180. Once in the air, pull back on the handlebars like you are doing a backflip. When you do the backflip and you are staring at the ground, turn your handlebars to the right hard and swing the tail of the bike out. Get your bearings and come back to earth. If you can't land it, you don't want it.

Back Flip

Speed is your friend on this one. Remember to keep your feet on the pedals as you take off. Pull up on the bars, look up and back, arch your back, and keep your eyes on the landing ramp. While in the air, keep your hands on the bars and your body in a low position. While you might be scared of not making it all the way around, going too far is just as bad. Over rotating and landing on your back wheel will cause you to bounce forward and faceplant over the bars.

Cliff Hanger

This one is cake. First, speed and air are needed. Lots of both. Once launched, take your feet off the pedals and hook them under the handlebars. Your arms go straight up above your head, giving the illusion that you are hanging from your toes off the front bars. Bring it all back down and land it. No prob.

360 Tailwhip

Here's another simple trick that will only take you, say, a hundred crashes to figure out. In the air, begin by spinning a 360. When you get 180 degrees around, spin your frame around with your feet, just like a regular tailwhip (see "Fly on Flatland"). Continue to spin. If you can figure out when you are at 360 degrees, catch your frame with your feet and put them down on the pedals. Land it and listen to the roar of the crowd. Don't land it and listen to silence.

WHO ARE THESE LUNATICS?

Some of the pro riders seem as if they are defying the laws of gravity. Their ability to make incredibly difficult moves look like a walk in the park is what amazes fans and judges alike. Even crazier is that most of these riders are just like you. Maybe a little bored, not really athletically endowed, and are the types who really would rather ride bikes with friends than pursue a more conventional form of work. Perhaps that is why the sport has taken off as of late. Other sports have created schisms between fans and athletes with images of zillion dollar contracts, and men and women with .005 percent body fat. Who relates to that? Here are some riders who still do their thing for the love of the sport.

Riding for Haro bikes is the street and vert legend Dave Mirra. He is responsible for so many tricks it's stupid. It has been said when he rides he looks like he is in a video game, it's so unreal. In fact, he even has his own video game. Barrel rolls, flairs, and no-handed 540s are all in his arsenal of moves. He's just too good. Also on the ramp is his good buddy Ryan Nyquist. His moves are also insane, with 720s and huge airs leading the way. A flat ground guy who shreds like mad is Gabe Weed. He adds new tricks often and is a real staple on the competition scene.

In terms of a bona fide hall of famer, everyone can agree that Mat Hoffman is the man. A force on the ramp for almost 15 years, he has now taken things to new heights, literally, with his newly built 24-foot tall quarter pipe. His goal was to nail 30 feet above the ramp. He needed a tow in on a YZ250 motorcycle. He hit 27 feet. He also hit his head on the landing, shattered his full-face helmet and was knocked out cold (27 foot air + 24 foot ramp = 51 foot fall). Can you taste the pain of that?

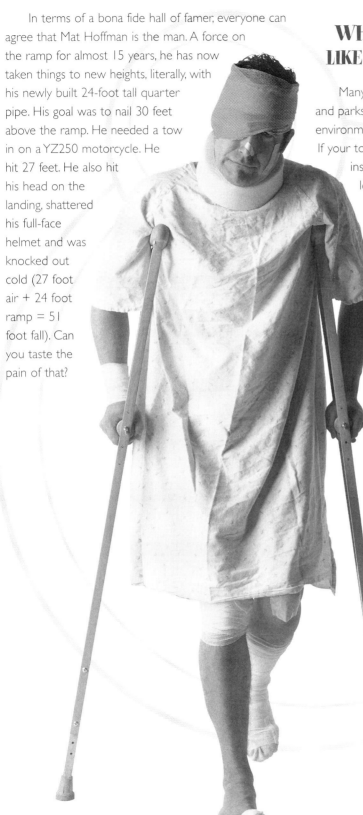

WHERE TO GO TO BE LIKE MAT HOFFMAN

Many towns today know that building ramps and parks will give kids a chance to practice in a safe environment away from angry cops and pedestrians. If your town has a park, go there to pick up on some instruction from other riders. For flatland, parking lots and driveways make good places, but you'll need to find people to ride with if you want to get good.

Other alternatives are the numerous freestyle camps popping up around the country, many of which are started by pro riders and cater to all levels and abilities. One of the best is Woodward Freestyle Camp in Pennsylvania. Run by superstar Dave Mirra, the camp offers instruction in all things freestyle and runs in the summer months. Dave even started a scholarship fund for those who can't find the coin to commit. Camps are simply a great way to develop skills on the bike while being surrounded by other like-minded riders.

Once the moves are down, it will be time to compete. In line with the ethos of freestyle, the competitions are less structured and have no real governing body. Visit your local shop or skatepark to find events to enter. Freestyle can get competitive, but it is not like racing. The vibe is much more fraternal, and riders generally tend to be very tight knit and support each other's abilities. If you are looking to crush someone in competition, maybe racing is for you. Freestyle is more an expression for those who have trouble articulating their purpose elsewhere. Once the language of 20-inch bikes is learned, it becomes clear what is being said. So stop asking so many questions and start riding.

3
MID-AIR
MADNESS

A h, there's nothing like the view of a big open sky—
especially when you're thousands of feet up, and you're
actually a falling dot in the great wild blue yonder. Yes, there
you are, with only a thin layer of fabric to counteract gravity's
darkest desire to bring you back down to earth faster than a
speeding watermelon, and with the same splatter factor.

Why would someone voluntarily jump out of an
airplane? Or jump from a bridge with a strip of elastic
attached to an
ankle? Or
surf the
updrafts of air
while inexorably
heading toward the
ground? Or jump off a
building? Whatever, the
rush is clearly on for
these sports.

Of course, there are other ways
to get high. Some people prefer the
relative serenity of gliding through
the sky. Air whooshes by, the
bustle of everyday life passes
well below your hang glider
or paraglider, and the
next thing you know...uh,
are those Chinese down there?

There are Xtremes out there for both kinds of thrill
seekers, and they can give you a lift if you keep reading.

TAKE A DIVE

For many years, skydiving was considered an Xtreme sport almost unto itself. There simply weren't many activities (other than dating, that is) that had you confronting questions such as: Can I face my fear? Do I believe in myself? Do I trust my equipment? Do I have guts? Am I going to die?

Now for many Xtremers, skydiving is considered almost casual fun.

LONG AGO

For the pioneers of sport parachuting, the object was, at first, merely to experience the thrill of leaping from a plane and surviving. Later, they made a sport of landing their parachutes as close to a target as possible, and these competitions are still held today.

Increasingly, however, the parachute ride came to be incidental to the real fun, which was the period of freefall from the moment the jumpers exited the airplane until they opened their canopies 2,000 feet above the ground. The change of emphasis led to a change of name, and "parachuting" became "skydiving."

According to the Federation Aeronautique Internationale, in 1998 there were 540,000 licensed skydivers worldwide, who made 5,563,000 skydives during that year. Americans made 3,400,000 skydives. This includes a quarter of a million jumps made by student-jumpers just being introduced to the sport.

There are literally thousands of skydiving drop zones (DZs) scattered across North America and the world. To get started, look in the yellow pages under "parachuting" or "skydiving." Most drop zones that offer training are affiliated with the United States Parachute Association (USPA). Plan to make your first jump in fair weather. Depending on where you live, this may mean waiting until late spring, summer, or early fall. But schedule an appointment. Making that commitment will solidify your resolve to jump.

Reputable, safety-conscious people run most skydiving companies. They've taken the plunge and want to help you experience the thrill they've had. For some, skydiving becomes a lifelong passion. They live for the next dive from a plane, escalating the experience by jumping from higher altitudes and attempting trickier maneuvers in freefall. Like most extreme sports, skydiving provides an adrenaline rush that translates into excitement and euphoria, especially after that first successful landing. The key word here is successful.

LEARNING TO FALL

First timers can expect to pay around $200 to $300 for a "maiden voyage" into the wild blue yonder. Subsequent jumps are often considerably less expensive, but this will never be a cheap sport. Reputable parachuting outfits will provide at least a half day of intensive classroom and on-the-ground instruction before suiting you up and loading you in an aircraft (weather permitting) for your first fateful jump. Jumpers are expected to sign liability release waivers and medical fitness declarations, and must be at least 18 years of age. Those weighing more than 250 pounds may be unable to jump safely. Ask your drop zone for details. Jumpers should dress appropriately for the weather, in non-restrictive clothing. Flexible athletic shoes are highly recommended.

During classroom and ground instruction, you will be introduced to the equipment. Modern parachutes are rectangular "ram-air" canopies; when opened they fill with air and become, essentially, inflated wings. They are highly maneuverable and have a forward speed of between 15 to 40 mph.

Parachutes come in various sizes. The smaller the parachute, the faster it descends. "Skygods" like to come in as fast as a glider, but more conservative jumpers take things slower. A common rule of thumb for beginners is: Don't jump a chute that is smaller in square feet than your weight, with gear. A 170 pound beginning jumper with 20 pounds of gear should jump no chute smaller than 190 square feet.

A skydiver wears his parachutes, main and reserve, in a backpack called a container. A container with gear in it is known as a rig. The main canopy (another name for the chute) is packed in a small bag at the bottom of the container. When a jumper wants to open the parachute, he releases a small parachute called a pilot chute, which has taken the place of the ripcord among serious jumpers. The pilot chute pulls the bag containing the main parachute out of the container, gradually unfolds the lines attaching it to the jumper's shoulders, and finally pulls the bag off the canopy, allowing it to catch the air and unfurl. This chain reaction makes the parachute deploy slowly, thereby decreasing the potential injury to the jumper and malfunction of the parachute.

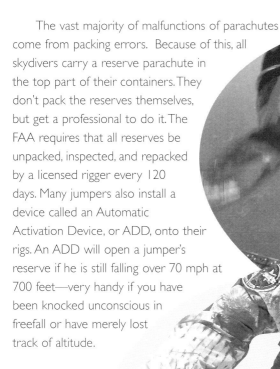

The vast majority of malfunctions of parachutes come from packing errors. Because of this, all skydivers carry a reserve parachute in the top part of their containers. They don't pack the reserves themselves, but get a professional to do it. The FAA requires that all reserves be unpacked, inspected, and repacked by a licensed rigger every 120 days. Many jumpers also install a device called an Automatic Activation Device, or ADD, onto their rigs. An ADD will open a jumper's reserve if he is still falling over 70 mph at 700 feet—very handy if you have been knocked unconscious in freefall or have merely lost track of altitude.

TAKING THE PLUNGE

No one will force you to jump should you lose your nerve; there's no shame in not bailing. Indeed, it's far better to lose your nerve on the ground or in the back of the plane than to hesitate at the point of no return. Accidents are far more likely to result from fits of last-minute panic than equipment failure. Just remember this: If you are confident, nothing will go wrong—your own self-confidence is your greatest insurance against most mishaps. Trust in yourself and all will go well. In any event, the choice will always be yours. This isn't the military, and you're not a queasy paratrooper facing disgrace. When it comes down to it, some jittery jumpers find they just don't have the nerve to climb out on a strut high above the clouds and simply let go.

But many do, and they're almost always glad they did. As a precaution against novice jumper error, your main chute will be attached to a static line, which is attached to the aircraft. It will automatically pull your ripcord within seconds of exiting the aircraft.

Novices rarely jump from altitudes above 3,000 to 4,000 feet. This is certainly a dizzying height, especially when viewed from the open door of a small aircraft, but experienced solo jumpers routinely skydive from 10,000 feet or more.

ASSUME THE POSITION

Upon letting go, you will assume the classic dive position: arms and legs extended and spread apart, belly down, head

1, 2, 3

up, back arched. You will be expected to count to ten. You will experience a moment of freefall before you feel an abrupt jerk as your chute opens above you. If you do not feel this jerk by the count of ten, you will be expected to *look at your pack*, grab its release control, and deploy the chute manually. If you have kept your wits about you, and have followed instructions, you will now experience an extraordinary sensation of floating peacefully in mid-air. Although you continue to descend, the sensation is one of virtual stillness and unearthly silence. You will have plenty of time to look above you at the vanishing plane. Looking down, the distant earth will appear serene and almost surreal.

You will probably have been instructed to land at a given destination. Often a type of bull's-eye is provided as an ideal target within the larger area of the landing site. You may have been provided with a helmet radio, through which you will receive advice from a ground-based dive instructor who is monitoring your progress.

STEER

The jumper steers with toggles that attach to the back of the canopy.

Modern chutes feature controls that will enable you to steer. Gently grasping the handles, you can experiment with these devices. By tugging gently on the right control you release a degree of captured air out of the right side of the canopy, forcing the parachute to bank to the right, and vice versa. With a little trial-and-error you will quickly comprehend how to steer.

By now you will notice that the once-distant ground is beginning to take shape below, and you may notice that it is approaching at an uncomfortable rate. If you have not already done so, it's time now to locate the landing target. If you jumped at (or very near to) the precise moment that you were instructed to do so, you should have no trouble locating the target. If you clung for dear life long after the jumpmaster shouted for you to go, you may find yourself far from the intended target. You've already overflown the target, and have no time to lose in locating and reaching it.

WHAT GOES UP...

As a jumper lands, he pulls down both toggles in what is known as a "flare," converting forward speed to lift and allowing him to land gently on his feet. In principle, that is; in practice, there are plenty of less-than-perfect landings and those wearing the dirty jumpsuits are there to prove it. That's because landing can be trickier than it looks.

You will be firmly instructed to *not* look down as the ground rushes up. The urge to do so is instinctual and strong. Whether you obey this instruction, you will hit the earth soon enough. Ideally, with knees bent, you will make contact and roll forward onto your thighs and shoulders as you have been trained to do. The idea is to absorb the shock of impact. Landing with a parachute is comparable to the impact of jumping from a height of about 10 feet. Clearly, it is not that great a leap, but it requires you to land with deeply bent knees. More than a few broken ankles have resulted from too-stiff landings.

You are now expected to get up as quickly as possible and gather your chute before any winds grab it and create a hopeless tangle. This is especially important on windy days or if you have over-shot the

target and have landed in less-than-ideal terrain. Novice jumpers have been known to allow their chutes to drag them over rocks and other obstacles, exposing them to worse injuries than any caused by the jump itself.

Upon successful completion of your first jump you will probably be either speechless with awe, or bursting with shouts of glee. After shucking your jump suit you will likely be presented with a certificate declaring your status as a first-time skydiver. Welcome to the club!

SPLAT, OR WHAT CAN GO WRONG

Needless to say, skydiving is not nearly as safe as needlepoint, but the risks are actually minimal. Of course,

there have been some extremely well publicized mishaps, usually with gory glumps of jumpers plastered across the evening news.

As mentioned previously, your biggest obstacle to a safe jump is likely to be your own mental fortitude. The vast majority of accidents, especially among beginners, can be attributed to jumper error. Jumpers will grab for the doorframe moments after jumping, or forget to "assume the position." When their chute deploys, it gets tangled and tragedy can result. Again, confidence and a strict adherence to the simple instructions received during exhaustive training will assure a safe, exhilarating jump.

Other possible sources of error include improperly packed chutes and airplane mechanical failures. There's little you can do about either. You will have to believe that the skydiving experts in whom you have placed your trust know what they are doing. You may eventually learn to fold and pack your own chute, firmly placing nearly all variables in your own capable hands. Until then, have faith.

FREEFALL ACTIVITIES

After doing 10 or 20 jumps, most jumpers find that the mere thrill of jumping, falling, and landing begins to wear off, and, as their level of comfort increases, that time in freefall can be filled with something more than sight-seeing.

In freefall dives, parachutists exit an aircraft at about 10,000 feet and experience about 30 seconds of freefall. During the first 10 seconds, a skydiver will accelerate to about 115-130 mph before deploying his chute at about 4,000 to 4,500 feet. The freefall speed record stands in excess of 300 mph.

When a body moves at such a high speed, small changes in the body's angles can make it move in different directions. When two

jumpers are falling together, these small changes make them move relative to each other—forward, backward, up, down. This is the traditional way to spend time in freefall and is called relative work, or RW.

Before a relative work jump, several jumpers will practice a formation on the ground, going over different combinations of hand and leg holds. They look like they're rehearsing a dance, and that's just what a well-executed RW jump is like in the air. Freefall skills take a long time to master (you get to practice for only a minute at a time) and every jumper has been on some disastrous jumps, where everyone flew around at random for the whole freefall. But a good team of jumpers can score an astonishing number of points (each formation is one point) in a single jump—some of the best teams can get 30 points in 30 seconds. A dive with two participants is called a two-way; three is a three-way, etc.

Not everyone goes for traditional RW. Some jumpers prefer sky surfing, which is discussed in depth later in this chapter. Sky surfing is not for the novice; the board is challenging to control, and only very experienced jumpers should try jumping with one.

THE SKY'S THE LIMIT

If you get hooked on skydiving, there's almost no limit to what you can aspire to do. Clubs around the world focus on stunt diving, relative work, and what is known as canopy formation skydiving (CFS).

TOP 5 Skydiving Movies

- Drop Zone
- Terminal Velocity
- From Wings Came Flight
- Angel, Angel, Down We Go
- The Skydivers

WHAT TO YELL ON THE WAY DOWN:

- Geronimo!
- Look, Ma, no wings!
- Parachutes? We don't need no stinking parachutes!
- Hey, I can see Rosie O'Donnell from here!
- Ahhhhhhhhhhhhhhhhhhhh!
- There must be a better way to sneak in to Disney World!
- I hope the ground will be friends with me!
- I'm the king of the world!
- Bombs away!
- Oh, God, what have I done!?

SURF'S UP...
WAY, WAY UP

Even among Xtreme sports crazies, sky surfing is considered extra extreme. Forget about simply jumping out of an airplane. That's not thrilling enough for sky surfers; they bail out with a sort of modified snowboard strapped to their feet. These airborne thrill seekers perform intricate acrobatics in an accelerating freefall. Upside-down, or right-side-up, twisting, pirouetting, looping, and barrel rolling, they surf the air at speeds of more than 100 mph, like a hurricane-propelled surfer hanging ten in the water, or a jet-equipped skateboarder cruising across concrete. Of course, the fall for the sky surfer is a little bit farther.

Airborne experience is a must for this sport. Long before they consider strapping on a sky board, sky surfers have already logged at least 100 or even 400 regular freestyle jumps, and are exceptionally skilled. The pros acknowledge the difference between a freestyle jump and sky surfing.

"You're actually going faster [in sky surfing]," says Sherry L. Schrimsher, former president of the United States Parachuting Association. "You're doing a combination of ballet, gymnastics, and dance in the air. There are a lot of g-forces and centrifugal forces being generated in different directions…there's a lot to watch out for."

A LITTLE HISTORY

Pioneered in (where else?) California in the early 1980s, sky surfing started with gutsy daredevils skydiving with Styrofoam surf boards, which they would lie on while grasping the boards' edges, like a traditional surfer paddling out to catch a wave. (It was called "air surfing" back then.)

Toward the end of the decade, ever more daring skydivers had graduated to standing up on modified boards that had been custom fitted with snowboard bindings. Each brief freefall brought new tries with aerial maneuvers, such as the "pinwheel" and "avalanche" (see Key Terms, page 78). Eventually, boards decreased in surface area, bindings became adjustable straps, and quick release mechanisms provided increased safety. Sky surf boards came to more closely resemble skateboards than traditional surfboards.

Since the early 1990s, the sport has attracted increased attention. Television commercials featuring breathtaking exhibitions of sky surfing prowess have raised the profile of the sport and inspired more skydiving enthusiasts to take the next leap. Although it may seem effortless to drink a soft drink

Risks are huge, and margin for error is slim. Hurtling head-down two miles above the earth requires a cool demeanor and quick reflexes. Spinning out of control like a whirling propeller—in a dangerous spiral called the flat spin—can scramble the senses and unnerve even the steeliest skydivers.

while hurtling through space on a board, the reality is assuredly not so simple.

ESPN's X Games put the sport in its lineup of envelope-pushing feats right from the games' inception in 1995. To score in that competition, surfers must make four 50-second jumps from approximately 10,500 feet. They jump in tandem with a cameraman, who must capture the contestant's spirals, spins, flips, and acrobatics. Top teams proceed to a final round of two jumps.

Activities More Dangerous than Sky Surfing

- Untamed shark-back riding
- Russian Roulette with six bullets
- Playing "chicken" against a 747
- Poking crocodiles with matchsticks
- Aggravating O.J. Simpson
- Jumping without a parachute
- Opening a business to compete with Microsoft

GEARING UP

In sky surfing, the lighter the gear the better. Lightweight boards are essential because they are easier to control at speeds of 120 mph. Sky surfers can expect to pay from about $500 to $700 for a custom designed board. Boards range from about four pounds to about eight pounds and are custom made to suit an individual's height, weight, and skill level. Don't skimp. As Dallas skydiving instructor T.J. Landgren says: "The more you spend on the board, the better."

Boards are made from composite materials, including aluminum, graphite, and Kevlar. Some brands incorporate an ingenious honeycomb interior, which ensures maximum structural strength, stability, and minimum weight. Boards are equipped with a binding system that's designed to release the board from a diver's feet in emergencies, such as the flat spin. (The emergency release mechanism also requires modifications to standard jumpsuit pants.) Boards include a small parachute if they must be released in midair. The board's recovery chute makes it easier to find and protects bystanders on the ground from being bonked by a board moving at missile speed.

Many sky surfers also carry a reserve parachute, an altimeter, an audible device to sound a warning when the diver reaches a certain altitude, a device for cutting away the board and the main chute (in case rigging gets tangled), and an automatic activation device for the reserve. This last gadget senses changes in altitude and opens the chute at a certain height, an extremely useful option if a jumper is knocked unconscious or otherwise disabled and can't manually deploy his parachute.

Most drop zones (DZs) will require beginning sky surfers to wear hard crash helmets. Tight fitting pants and a jumpsuit are also recommended. Shoes should be low-topped, lace-up athletic shoes, and pants must be modified to accommodate the Velcro cutaway handle attachment for quick release of the board in an emergency.

Sky surfers will need a square reserve and a bottom-of-container (BOC) main parachute system. Some sky surfing experts prefer a pullout deployment (POD) parachute container system, which reduces the chance of the pilot chute inadvertently opening. Boards should not exceed 11-inches in width; anything wider may create air turbulence and cause the pilot chute to deploy unexpectedly.

GETTING STARTED

Sky surfer wannabes must first become exceptionally proficient, licensed skydivers with plenty of freefall experience, and the documentation to prove it, before reputable DZs will consider allowing them to attempt a sky surfing jump. Most DZs require at least 100 jumps and recommend as many as 400 before a skydiver applies for sky surf training. As San Francisco skydiving instructor Patrick Wilson says, "Attaching a board to your feet is a very serious proposition."

A prospective sky surfer should have his own beginner board and should have carefully viewed the instructional video that came with the board. Ten to 50 free fly dives, including sit fly and standup maneuvers, are required, and head down free fly dives are recommended. Likewise, DZs will insist that you complete at least five to ten beginner sky surfing dives before advancing to an intermediate board.

OTHER VENUES

In 1995, the International Parachuting Commission incorporated freestyle skydiving, including sky surfing, into its activities. The commission created the World Freestyle Federation (WFF) to set competition rules and to organize freestyle and sky surfing competitions. The first world championships for sky surfing were held in Efes, Turkey, in 1997. In 1998, the second world championships were held in Corowa, Australia. World championships for freestyle skydiving and sky surfing were held at the World Air Games in Granada, Spain, in June 2001.

KEY TERMS

As if sky surfing weren't hard enough, it also has a jargon all its own.

Avalanche: Invented by Troy Hartman, this is a spin initiated by grabbing the back of the sky surf board and tumbling forward.

Backflip: A backward pinwheel—heels over head.

Backloop: A single backflip.

Bottom of Container (BOC): A type of parachute container design in which the pilot chute is tucked into a pouch located at the bottom of the backpack. Less popular with sky surfers than POD (see entry), due to the possibility that the pilot chute could inadvertently deploy in extreme jumps at high speeds ranging from 140 to 180 mph.

Head down position

Cartwheel: A sideways spin initiated by pulling one arm down to the side while extending one arm out; much like a gymnastic cartwheel on the ground.

Flat spin: A dangerous, unwanted spin in which the jumper rotates while on his belly. Imagine the body spinning around an axis through the belly button, like a helicopter propeller. Due to increasing centrifugal forces, blood rushes to the extremities and can cause eyeball hemorrhaging, or worse. If this spin is not controlled within the first three to four seconds, the skysurfer must release his board to stop the spin. If he waits too long, it may become impossible to do so and the jumper may crash.

Head down: Opposite of stand up; jumper freefalls while in head-down position.

Layout: Consecutive backflips (two or more in a row).

Pinwheel: A front loop maneuver, in which a surfer grabs the front of the board and spins head over heels back to an upright position.

Pull Out Deployment (POD): A parachute container that features a handle that connects by a strap to the pilot chute, which is packed in the backpack with the main chute. Since the pilot is not contained in an external pouch, there is less danger of inadvertent deployment, and less danger of flaps of material catching air at an inopportune time.

Relative work: Refers to jumps in which several skydivers jump simultaneously and are fairly close to one another while in freefall. The divers create mid-air formations by linking hands, feet, etc. You've probably seen this type of thing in movies or on TV. Elaborate relative work can involve 20 or more divers linked in a geometric formation; think synchronized swimming or chorus line dancers forming patterns in the sky.

Sit fly: A skydiving maneuver in which a jumper assumes a sitting position while in the air, with back erect, legs out and bent at the knees about 90 degrees, as if sitting in a chair. Teaches the use of the hands and back as controlling mechanisms, a prerequisite to sky surfing.

Slipstream sit-suit: A skydiving jumpsuit designed with extra flaps of material on the upper arms; winglets designed to catch air and make the sit fly maneuver easier to do. Considered sort of "training wheels" for those learning to sit fly.

Square reserve: A square-canopy reserve parachute.

Stand up: The jumper stands upright while in freefall.

BASE JUMPING

There may come a time when you might simply want to hurl yourself at the ground. You might want to climb up a mountain or some other high place and dive right off, a parachute on your back, which, when you pull the ripcord, snatches you from the jaws of death. At times like that—and don't we all have them—you want to BASE jump: "Building," "Antenna," "Span," (such as a bridge over a deep gorge or river), and "Earth," (a mountain or cliff)—all tall enough, and this is key, to give a parachute time to open.

BASE jumping is the sport of leaping off a fixed object; it's similar to skydiving, and many BASE jumpers are also skydivers. But BASE offers jumpers unique challenges and sensations that skydivers don't experience. For one, jumping off a fixed object gives that "falling" feeling—the rush of acceleration as you plummet to your death—that skydivers (who are already moving in the airplane at 80 mph when they jump) don't feel. And BASE jumpers regularly experience "ground rush," the sight of the ground visibly, quickly, and inexorably approaching; ground rush is a phenomenon that starts below 1,000 feet, and skydivers try very hard not to be in a free fall that low. In fact, a skydiver considers a jump from 2,000 feet "low," while BASE jumpers routinely leap off objects that are only a few hundred feet tall. This doesn't afford much time to sight see; if you don't do everything just right, you stand a very good chance of dying or at least hurting yourself very badly.

BASE jumping demands near-perfect canopy control and landing skills. A typical BASE jump has a landing area that is filled with boulders, rocks, and large trees on an uneven terrain. Fixed objects also create their own special wind conditions, which are usually turbulent and unpredictable—there's no convenient wind sock to tell you which way to land.

BASE jumpers need excellent freefall skills, too. It is very important to launch your body in such a way that you fly away from the object; otherwise, you stand a chance of hitting it when opening your parachute. For the same reason, it's crucial to pack your canopy so that it doesn't spin you around and slam you straight into a cliff face.

In case you haven't surmised it by now, BASE jumping is a very dangerous sport—many highly skilled and well-respected jumpers have died doing it. It is also often illegal; many jumpers have been arrested or had their gear confiscated by angry property owners or park rangers. Perhaps the most important skill a BASE jumper needs is good judgment and an instinct for when to go or when to back out of a jump. It's too dangerous an activity to let someone else make up your mind for you. If a little voice in your head says that today is not a good day, listen to it.

GEAR

If you're feeling the insane urge to try this sport, don't grab a skydiving rig and just go for it. Although BASE jumpers often use skydiving gear, they make important modifications to reflect the unique conditions of low-altitude jumps. BASE jumpers use parachutes bigger than the ones favored by skydivers; most skydivers use small

nine-cell canopies, but BASE jumpers use giant 7-cell chutes, which open wider and capture more air faster. BASE canopies are also rigged differently and packed differently from skydiving parachutes. BASE canopies usually are attached to enormous pilot chutes. This enables the main parachute to open rapidly. (Skydivers actually expend a lot of energy coming up with ways to make their canopies open more slowly.)

BASE jumpers generally don't carry a reserve or automatic activation device inside their rigs. What would be the point? BASE jump altitudes give you time to open one parachute, and usually there's no second chance.

Oddly, BASE rigs are often not the nicest or newest pieces of equipment. In this sport, there's always the chance that you might have to abandon your gear and run for it from the authorities; you'd hate to do that with an expensive rig. In recent years, some companies have begun marketing BASE-specific rigs. These are big chutes designed to hold only one canopy (no reserve), and are often held closed only by Velcro, to ensure faster openings.

TRAINING

The first thing to do if you want to get into BASE jumping is to learn to skydive. Go to your local "drop zone," enroll in a first-jump course, and make a bunch of jumps. Skydiving is way cool and well worth learning for its own sake, and you may find that you no longer desperately want to jump off fixed objects. And virtually every skill you learn at the drop zone will stand you in good stead if you decide to BASE jump. In particular, work on canopy control and accuracy, and learn as much as you can about packing and rigging. Use skydives to get used to your gear. The middle of the sky at 6,000 feet is the best place to test packing techniques and pull positions; you want to have perfect openings down pat long before you really need them.

Once you've got a handle on skydiving (remember, most BASE jumpers recommend doing at least 200 skydives first), find a local BASE jumper and offer to ground crew some jumps for him; generally get to know your local BASE jumping community. Go to events, such as Bridge Day (see page 82) and either watch, volunteer, or if you are ready, jump.

If after all this, you are still sure that you want to learn to BASE jump, find someone to teach you. Don't try to teach yourself this sport; the knowledge of those who have gone before you and are alive to tell about it is invaluable and could save your life. If you can't find a local or area BASE jumper, you could take a first-jump course with one of the gear manufacturers, such as Basic Research or Consolidated Rigging.

For example, Basic Research offers a BASE jumping course that includes two full days of classroom instruction, and a jump day. Students spend their evenings working on packing and other skills and watching a huge number of videos. Topics include site analysis, weather considerations, launch mechanics, gear

Make Your Skydive Now!

on a Miles-High Tandem Skydive

photo by Brian Erler

maintenance, rigging and malfunctions, and legal issues. Students must be at least 18 and have already made at least 150 parachute jumps. The class is kept small, two or three students at a time, and costs $1,000, which includes equipment. For the jumping day, students generally jump out of a hot air balloon tethered at 600 feet; this allows students to make several jumps in a day.

A balloon is safer, too, than a cliff or building, since there is nothing to hit between launching and landing. Real BASE jumps are also possible, for an additional fee. Basic Research also offers advanced training trips several times during the year, which gives course graduates an opportunity to further improve their skills.

POPULAR BASE JUMP SITES

One of the most popular legal BASE jump events is the yearly Bridge Day at New River Gorge, West Virginia. The bridge of the New River Gorge is 876 feet high. On Bridge Day, the third Saturday in October, BASE jumping is legal from 9:00 a.m. until 3:00 p.m., and during that time the jumps are fast and furious. There are a limited number of places available, so jumpers must register in advance. The landing area is small and rocky, and varies in size depending on the river's level. Boats patrol the river below the bridge to pick up anyone who doesn't quite make it to dry land. There are some spectacular jumps done every year, including large group launches and aerial acrobatics.

Angel Falls in Venezuela is another popular BASE jumping destination. It is the tallest waterfall in the world at 3,212 feet, and is located in the midst of dense jungle. The falls are in a national park, and just getting there is an adventure in itself. Angel Falls

jumpers usually go with a group organized by a leader who makes arrangements with Venezuelan park rangers and local jumpers. Jumps made this way are legal, and there's actually a helicopter transporting jumpers to the top of the falls.

A trip to Angel Falls isn't cheap, but it would certainly be a once-in-a-lifetime experience. Non-jumpers are welcome to make the journey and fly up to the top of Angel Falls for the view, which is indeed spectacular. Would-be Angel Falls jumpers need to be especially good at canopy control, since the landing area is a tiny space carved out of the rain forest every year when the jumpers arrive.

El Capitan in Yosemite National Park has near-legendary status in the BASE jumping community. Some trace the beginnings of the sport to a 1978 film by Carl Boenish of several BASE jumpers leaping from the summit. This film inspired more jumpers to visit the site, and although the National Park Service has banned the activity and jumpers get arrested every year, lots of BASE jumpers trek out there every year for the altitude and beauty of the site. Getting to the top requires a hike, and would-be jumpers are often hassled by park rangers who don't enjoy picking up dead bodies. Jumpers who get caught are fined and have their gear confiscated, and sometimes go to jail, too.

BUNGEE JUMPING

Imagine that you've spent weeks erecting a ramshackle tower, using only the wood and vines in the forest. With trepidation, you eye the platform that rises from the surrounding jungle and looms high above the treetops.

Soon you will scale its heights and plunge headfirst to earth.

The health and well being of the village and the success of the harvest must be insured. Only the dive from dizzying heights—the ancient ritual known as N'Gol—will satisfy the gods.

The earth beneath the tower has been turned over to soften your initial touchdown. You have carefully measured the verdant vines that you will soon trust with your life. The time has come to climb the tower to your perch. After tying the vines to your ankles, you say a few choice words for the benefit of the festive crowd below. You're all too aware that these words may be your last should the vines break, or if you have measured incorrectly. Perhaps you reflect for a moment on your ancestors—brave men—who have made similar dives before you.

Then you plunge into the void.

With luck, you scrape the rich earth with your shoulders, your strength and courage now touching the land. The crops will flourish. Your manhood is affirmed. With luck, your skull also remains intact, and you survive to walk away—perhaps to jump again, another season.

ANCIENT ROOTS AND MODERN BEGINNINGS

This jungle jump is an ancient ritual still practiced today by Pentecost Island tribesmen, in the remote South Pacific archipelago of Vanuatu. The modern world got its first glimpse of this ancient ritual in the mid-20th century during the broadcast of a televised documentary. The sight of near-naked men plunging to earth from rickety towers more than 100 feet tall sparked some people's imagination and set the stage for a new Xtreme sport that has since spanned the globe.

According to modern lore, a group of British sports enthusiasts known as the Oxford Dangerous Sports Club (DSC) was inspired by the telecast to emulate the risky feat on April 1, 1977. Defying gravity (and, arguably, common sense), club members sporting tuxedos tied elastic cords to their ankles and dove off a suspension bridge near Bristol, England. Although the daring April Fool's Day divers were promptly arrested, nothing could stop the craze that soon spread around the globe. Thus from humble roots in a primitive people's venerable ritual, the modern sport of bungee jumping was born.

Less than three decades after that first fateful jump, millions of people have taken the plunge—most under safe (and legal) conditions. Afterward, most report feelings ranging from euphoria and excitement to intense emotional release. Some people laugh uncontrollably, and some have been known to have a mini-Tourette's Syndrome-like outbreak during the jump. A.J. Hackett of New Zealand is widely credited with publicizing the sport; his insane jumps, including one from the Eiffel Tower, put bungee jumping at the top of the news.

Brothers John and Peter Kockelman of California are credited with importing the fledgling sport to the United States in the late 1980s. The rock-climbing duo pioneered the use of precise calculations and special equipment to insure safety. By the early 1990s commercial venues sprang up across North America. Although the sport was banned in some countries after a spate of accidents, improvements in safety have helped make the sport popular worldwide. Commercial jump operations now make use of everything from cranes and towers to hot air balloons, helicopters, and gondola cars as launch platforms.

The Eiffel Tower, Paris

WHAT ARE THE RISKS?

Some serious injuries and deaths have been associated with the sport. But, according to a 1998 report published in the medical journal *The Physician and Sport Medicine*, bungee jumping under controlled conditions is "relatively safe." The report was based on a study, which evaluated the experiences of 100 jumpers who plunged from a height of 130 feet with bungee cords attached to their ankles. About three-fourths of the jumpers in the study were males; the jumpers' average age was 26. Professional jump companies note, though, that their clients range from the relatively young (most impose a minimum age of at least 12) to people over 65.

The most common complaint associated with jumping is dizziness. Proponents of the sport point out that the sensation is only natural, considering that jumpers spend a minute or more suspended head down. Other common complaints include temporary blurred vision and minor skin burns. More serious complaints include lacerations and other traumas, including spinal cord damage and asphyxiation.

But enthusiasts point out that injuries are almost always the result of human error, rather than equipment failure. Injuries also appear to be more common among acrobatic jumpers. Minor injuries often result when panicked jumpers experience a change of heart immediately after the point of no return. Attempts to grab the rope or platform—despite clear instructions to drop headfirst and to keep your hands free—contribute to injuries.

BETTER SAFE THAN SORRY

Safety is, of course, a major concern for everyone involved in this Xtreme sport. In most venues, states or other government entities strictly regulate jumping. Reputable jump operators provide instruction in proper jump technique, and their jump employees undergo rigorous training. In most cases, equipment is checked before and after every jump. Today's bungee cords consist of multiple strands of rubber and synthetic fibers.

First developed by the military, these modern elastic cords are designed to withstand repeated use, and to absorb the shock of sudden loads. Several factors are taken into account in order to launch a jumper safely. The jumper's weight must be measured, as well as the exact length and elasticity of the cords, and the height of the jump platform. Most jump

companies in North America use "the American style" system of multiple cords to both the jumper and the tower. In theory one set of cords will prevent disaster in the unlikely event of another cord failing.

Some jump outfits take the additional precaution of placing an inflated landing pad below the jump site. Rock-climbing inspired harnesses serve as attachments between jumper and tower. Cords may be attached to the ankles, but this original method is now often reserved for more experienced jumpers. The safest jump rigs use chest and torso harnesses.

JUMPING IN A NUTSHELL

If you're ready to take the plunge, you can expect to pay anywhere from $50 to $100 per jump for the privilege. Jump sites exist all over the world, from cranes or on old bridge pylons to specially modified hot air balloons and helicopters. There are even mobile, self-contained towers that are most commonly encountered at venues such as fairs and carnivals. Most commercial jumps involve heights ranging from 120 to 200 feet.

You will be expected to sign a waiver of liability and a statement of general good health. Minors will be required to have at least one parent or guardian sign a release form. Some operators require a minimum weight of at least 80 pounds, while special charges may apply to those weighing more than 250 pounds, due to the necessity of additional equipment. Jump operators may exclude anyone who is believed to be under the influence of drugs or alcohol.

After receiving instructions you will be weighed, then harnessed to jump gear. Upon launching, you will enter freefall; in the second phase of the jump you rebound (if all goes well). You are bounced upwards where you may experience a sense of weightlessness, similar to the sensation encountered on a fast-descending elevator (minus the elevator). After rebound you eventually stabilize and are retrieved and unharnessed. You did it.

JUMPING INTO THE FUTURE

Various innovations have been introduced to the sport in recent years, but they are not recommended for any but the most experienced jumpers. They include practices such as launching from the ground (aptly named "slingshoting") and "body dipping," in which jumps take place over bodies of water. If executed properly, this variation involves a stimulating dip into the water. If botched, spinal cord or head injuries—or drowning—could conceivably be the result.

"Sandbagging" involves jumping with a weight that is released at the bottom of the fall. The additional energy is transmitted to the rebound, slingshoting the jumper higher than is normally possible. Daring innovators also engage in acrobatics while in freefall, performing somersaults, twists and other gymnastic moves. But, again, these embellishments on the basic bungee jumping experience are absolutely not recommended for the inexperienced. That's you.

Most Popular Places to Bungee Jump

> Cranes
> Bridges
> Buildings with platforms
> Towers
> Hot air balloons
> Helicopters
> Cable Cars
> Catapults

Types of Bungee Jumps

Body harness jump
Leg harness jump
Cutaway
Swallow dive
Slingshot
Sandbagging
Back dive
Railing jump
Thrown
Body dipping
Top of cage
Arm harness jump

KITE + SURF BOARD = KITESURFING

Kitesurfing (aka kiteskiing, kite boarding, flysurfing, or kitesailing) is a newbie sport, but one of the fastest growing of the Xtremes. The concept is simple: You strap your feet to a surfboard and hold on to a kite, which pulls you across the water. The reality is a lot more complicated and presents the sort of challenge Xtremites crave: Since the kite and the board are connected only by the surfer, he must control them both at the same time.

© Eric Sanford/Kite Boarding Magazine

© Bill Doster/Kite Boarding Magazine

traction kite can be much more powerful and create much faster speeds than a wind surfing sail. A sail uses available wind to generate power; but the lift of a kite is equal to the *square* of wind velocity, so a surfer will attain a speed that's a multiple of the wind speed. For example, a four-knot wind would equal 16 knots of lift. Even more fun would be a 12 knot wind, which would produce a 144 knot lift—actually more like liftoff.

(Also consider that surfing on water isn't the only use for traction kites. They can also be used in the winter on snow or ice, on land with a wheeled buggy, or on water with a boat.)

Kite flyers spent years dreaming about ways to replace conventional wind surfing sails with kites, but this wasn't feasible until manufacturers created kites that could be relaunched (get you back into the

TRACTION KITES

A kitesurfing kite is not exactly what you pick up at Safeway. You need a traction kite, which has multiple lines for precise control. A flying kite generates lift similar to an airplane; the bigger the kite, the greater the force. This means that a big enough kite easily has enough power to propel an object across the water.

Though kitesurfing resembles wind surfing, a

air after a fall) from the water. Two kites, Wipika and Kite Ski, were introduced in the 1980s; more recent additions to the field include FOne, Concept Air, C-Quad, and Naish kites. They employ different designs and vary in how easily they can be relaunched. Because the sport is still in its infancy, gear and techniques are changing rapidly every year.

With current equipment, a kitesurfer can get up and running in winds as low as four or five knots and as high as 40 or 50 knots. As equipment improves, it might become possible to kitesurf in even lighter winds.

A kitesurfer can launch the board from the shore or from the water. Generally no assistance is necessary to launch or land the kite, unless the kitesurfer is on a crowded beach.

SAFETY

Kitesurfing can be dangerous, but what Xtreme sport isn't? Some kitesurfing kites will keep flying even if the kitesurfer falls, which can present certain problems. You definitely don't want a kite dragging you out to sea or into rocks, or, God forbid, up in the air in very strong winds. A kitesurfer must be able to release the kite instantly. A deadman safety release system allows the kite to be disabled at any moment; most release the kite if the operator lets go of the control bar. It should go without saying that you should never attach the kite to yourself with any sort of permanent fastener.

On the continuum of dangerous sports, kitesurfing is safer than hang gliding but more dangerous than its cousin, wind surfing. At least one person has died kitesurfing, and the sport is only a few years old. However, there are many common sense precautions a kitesurfer can take that will minimize the risk of injury to himself or others. These include obvious safeguards such as wearing a helmet, life jacket, and wetsuit, never kitesurfing near power lines or airports, never kitesurfing in very strong winds, and never kitesurfing in crowded waters. Doing lots of pullups will also help by making your arms stronger and more able to control the kite.

GEAR

Okay, we'll admit it: One of the best reasons to get into kitesurfing is the cool gear you can buy. This includes a kite that can be relaunched from the water's surface, a kitesurf board, a kite control device, and multiple accessories, such as a board leash, a safety release system, a harness, life jacket, wetsuit, helmet, shoes and gloves, and whatever else you need to express your own personal style.

for a kite usually includes a control device, i.e., the lines that the pilot holds to steer the kite. Depending on kite style and personal preference, a kitesurfer can use a 2- or 4-line control bar or a pair of 4-line handles to control the kite.

© Eric Sanford/Kite Boarding Magazine

There are three main types of kites currently on the market. Inflatable kites have an inflatable leading edge and inflatable battens that give them a crescent moon or elliptical shape. Inflatable kites are probably the easiest to launch and relaunch, except in very light winds. Framed single-skin kites have a leading edge made of fiberglass or graphite, one main batten in the center, and a number of thin battens that give the kite a shape.

Although these kites take a lot of practice to launch, they are probably the most dependable for water relaunching; they are hard to launch in light winds. Ram-air foil kites (also called closed cell foil kites) have no rigid structure and function much like ram-air parachutes or airplane wings. They normally have a limited number of air intakes and a valve system to prevent air escaping from the kite after the kitesurfer falls; a safety release system is crucial with this kind of kite. Ram-air foil kites are known for their dependability and are quite popular with the kitesurfing community.

Kites cost between $500 and $1,200. The price

© Bill Doster/Kite Boarding Magazine

© Eric Sanford/*Kite Boarding Magazine*

between 60 and 80 feet; the longer the lines, the less wind that's necessary. Longer lines have a greater margin for pilot error, so they are best for beginners. The kitesurfing authorities generally recommend that kitesurfers use lines with a strength of at least 2.5 times the surfer's weight; e.g., a 200 lb. kitesurfer should use 500 lb. lines. Recommended line strength varies by kite and manufacturer.

Boards come in several styles: a surfboard style with foot straps, a wakeboard style with bindings, a pair of waterski-style skis with bindings, or anything else you can get to work. Choice of board depends on the kitesurfer's previous experience with board sports and the prevailing winds; bindings are advisable in high wind areas. Smaller kiteboards work best in high winds. All kiteboards have to be shorter than 8 feet; any larger and they would be difficult to steer upwind and might launch from the water. Boards can have from one to five fins, though most have two or three. A board runs between $500 and $900. It is possible to find used kitesurfing equipment, and some intrepid souls have made their own kites and converted their old surfboards into kiteboards.

Normally you only need one kiteboard. If you live in a light wind area (five to fifteen knots) with some high wind days (20 to 30+ knots), you may want to consider having two boards: a larger one for regular days and a smaller one for super-high-wind days.

A 2-line kite can turn left or right and go straight; this kind of kite is best for beginners because it is easy to control, less expensive, and less likely to get tangled. On a 4-line system, the front lines are called the main lines, and the back lines are called the brake lines. By pulling on various combinations of lines, a kitesurfer can turn left or right, spin the kite in the same spot, slow down, stop, or move backward. Four-line systems are also easier to relaunch from the water.

Most kites can fly in a wind of as little as four knots. Serious kitesurfers usually buy four kites to carry them through a wide range of wind speeds. The average length for lines is

© Bill Doster/*Kite Boarding Magazine*

For the best tips, techniques, and latest buzz on all things kite boarding, subscribe to *Kite Boarding Magazine* by calling 877-228-0027. Be sure to check out HYPERLINK http://www.kiteboardingmag.com, the official site of *Kite Boarding Magazine*.

GETTING STARTED

Kitesurfing obviously generates many comparisons with wind surfing. Kitesurfers say it is fairly easy to move from wind surfing to their sport, and that the two are complementary; board control skills are similar. Kitesurfers can have fun in lower winds and flatter waters, but wind surfing is safer and more fun than kitesurfing in high winds. Kiteboards are faster than sailboards going downwind but slower going upwind.

Learning to kitesurf is pretty easy, but beginners should be aware that there are several skills that you will want to master before you strap on a board and head out to sea. There are numerous rigs in both the two and four line varieties available from a growing number of reputable vendors. Once you have the rig, the first thing you should do is head to a beach and go fly your kite. Don't strap it into your rig yet, just get the hang of what it feels like. One of the first things you will have to learn is the "water launch."

While wind surfers take quite some time to work up to this, it's the most basic skill in kitesurfing, and it's required to get the kite off the ground. You'll launch by playing out your lines, and moving upwind from the starting position of your kite. For practice you'll do this on the beach, but you'll have to do it in the water once you're ready. As you play the lines out, you can adjust

the tension by feel. Once you have 60 feet (20m) of line (a good amount to start with) you can give the kite a little slack. The wind will start to fill the kite, and once it has filled it will quickly shoot skyward. When it's up, practice moving it around: left, right, up, down, in a curve. You'll quickly feel out how to do this through trial and error. Once you have the kite going, practice moving it left while you run to the right, and vice versa. Practice turning it into the wind while you run downwind. In general, get a feel for the way that the kite moves in the wind, and how you have to move in order to stay in sync with it. Then try some more athletic things. Lay down and practice letting the kite pull you up. See how far you can lean with the kite holding you up. This will teach you what the limitations of your movement are and what the kite can do

Once you have a sense of what basic handling feels like, you should try out the deadman release on your rig. You should never, ever, get into a rig without knowing how your deadman release works, and if it is in good working order.

© Eric Sanford/Kite Boarding Magazine

The next step is to better understand the thrust of your kite. The kite will generate the most power when it is perpendicular to the wind. But there are times when you don't want full power. Imagine a car with the throttle always open, and you get an idea of what you'd be in for if you didn't know how to control the power of the device. You can control the power of a four-line kite by changing the angle that the kite has relative to the wind direction. By changing the angle that the kite has relative to the direction of the wind, you decrease its available surface area, and thus the amount of power that it generates. You can generate a similar effect by using the brake lines.

Once you can maneuver your kite, control the pull and speed, and you know that your deadman release works, it's time to enter the water. Your first trips will be without a board, though. In shallow water, practice water launches of your kite. (The specifics of how to do this will vary depending on the type of kite you have and should be explained in the instructions that come with the kite.) Once you've got it up, let your kite pull you through the water, and practice maneuvering at these slower speeds. Get a feel for how the kite and the water work together. You'll also want to practice deep-water launches of your kite. This is an essential skill and one that you need to learn well and quickly.

Got all that? Good. We're ready to kitesurf. Wait for a day with moderate breezes of about 15 knots. This will give you enough wind that you don't have to fight to stay up, but not so much that you risk ending up in Australia. Now it's time to get on your board. Launch your kite, and put it directly overhead. Now walk out into knee to chest-deep water, past the breakers and get your feet into the bindings. The rear binding should be just back from the center of the board, the front binding should be far enough forward so that your feet will be shoulder width apart. You will now be lying on your back with your feet strapped in and the wind to your back. Dive the kite down. This will generate speed and a great deal of pull, which you will use to get yourself out of the water. You are better off starting slow and falling backwards rather than having too much pull and face planting— you'll have to unstrap and start over in the latter case. In the former, you can just sail your kite back up and begin again. Once you have pulled out, you'll want to play with your kite and your balance. The essentials, though, are to keep your feet planted and your weight just to the back of the center of the board. You'll fly the kite at about 75 degrees up from the water to get moving; if you need more power, dive it.

Now comes the hard part. Staying up. Don't worry, you won't. This will be frustrating, but you have to learn somehow. If you can't seem to get it together, go back to the beach and keep practicing until your kite control becomes second nature. The biggest obstacle to overcome is the uncertainty that comes with trying to

© Eric Sanford/Kite Boarding Magazine

do two unfamiliar things at the same time. Once you're moving, though, just keep the following basics in mind. Your kite will need to fly at about 30-45 degrees depending on wind speed. Keep your knees bent for better balance. Learn how far you can lean into a turn. Learn to watch your kite, not your feet. Master that, and you'll be flying off the wave-tops in no time.

Kitesurfers say that their sport is easier to learn than wind surfing. There are a number of kitesurfing schools cropping up across the globe, and some devotees have traveled to study with the pioneers of the sport, such as Cory Roeseler and Laurent Ness. You can also find instructional videos and a lot of advice on the Internet. There are tons of kitesurfing discussion groups on the Web, easily located through search engines. There are also a number of Web sites dedicated to the sport, many of which provide lists of schools and gear providers.

REGULATION

There is not yet a governing body for the sport of kitesurfing, and so the sport is basically unregulated. The Professional Air Sports Association, founded in 1997, is a non-profit organization that is trying to incorporate councils from a number of air sports, including hang gliding, paragliding, parasailing, and kitesurfing. PASA has been setting standards for instruction in all these sports, and has established an instructor certification program for kitesurfing. It is trying to develop a nationally recognized level of certification, in an effort to provide quality control in kitesurfing training.

The Kitesurfing International Safety System (K.I.S.S.) is trying to set worldwide standards for kitesurfing instructors and schools, protecting the future of the sport by promoting safe practices, providing a course of study for novice kitesurfers, and certifying trainers. K.I.S.S. techniques were developed in Hawaii by kitesurfing pioneers and are now being taught all over the world.

© Bill Doster/*Kite Boarding Magazine*

PARAGLIDING

BACKGROUND

Paragliding is another fledgling sky sport, developed mainly during the 1980s. As aviation sports go, this one is as safe as it gets. Crashes are virtually non-existent among certified paragliders, though there have been incidents among "self-taught" pilots. (We hope this reinforces the importance of learning to fly from a qualified instructor.) The safety of the sport is particularly visible in Europe where paragliding is wildly popular, and entire families will paraglide together, kids to grandparents. The sport is similar to hang gliding (see pages 99-102), but paragliders are slower, easier to control, and weigh much less.

In addition to being a safe and relatively easy skill to master, paragliding has the advantage of not requiring a particular terrain type or a dedicated park. All you need is a rig and some clear airspace. Steep hills or mountains are not required; there are paragliding groups everywhere from Aspen to Miami. Worldwide, there are paragliding groups and vacation tours in India, South Africa, Australia, Scotland, and just about any place else there is open sky and a breeze.

World Records of Paragliding:

- Straight distance—
  202.2 mi. by Godfrey Wenness
- Straight distance to a declared goal—
  155.5 mi. by Alex François Louw
- Out-and-return distance—
  105.6 mi. by Pierre Bouilloux
- Distance over a triangular course—
  126.5 mi. by Klaus Heimhofer
- Speed over a 15.5 mi. triangular course—
  17.6 mph by Patrick Berod
- Speed over a 31 mi. triangular course—
  14.7 mph by Enda Murphy
- Speed over a 124.3 mi. triangular course—
  14.6 mph by Klaus Heimhofer
- Speed over a 62.1 mi. out-and-return course—
  17.4 mph by Howard Travers

GEAR

There are three main parts to a paraglider: the risers, or the cords, which suspend the pilot; the harness, which supports the pilot; and the canopy. The canopy is a lightweight, soft, parachute-like device. You've seen paragliders high above—bright colors dotting the sky. There's a reason for the flashy spectrum. Some colors are more resistant to ultra-violet light. Red, orange, purple, dark blue, white, and black are the best.

You'll shell out anywhere from $3,000 to $5,000 for your paraglider and harness. The size of the glider will depend on your height and weight. And besides being expensive, paragliding equipment is delicate. Remember: A hot asphalt surface can damage the fabric, as can even car or motorcycle exhaust.

Even with careful use, wear and tear is to be expected. The good news is a canopy can be cleaned and repaired. A small tear won't reduce a wing's resistance if it is repaired by a specialist. Regularly inspecting the canopy is a good idea.

For cleaning, use water and a mild detergent for stains or marks. Do not scrub the cloth. And be sure not to get your lines wet, or they might shrink. When your glider is completely dry, pack it up. With proper maintenance, most gear will last about four years.

One of the best things about the paraglider itself is its compactness. All that material fits nicely into a knapsack-sized bundle weighing between 20 and 30 pounds.

Also remember that when you're ready to fly, the temperature will generally fall about five degrees Fahrenheit with every 1,000 feet of ascent. That means it might be 75 degrees on the ground and a chilly 60 at 3,000 feet. Climbing boots with a low heel, a full length windsuit or jeans, a sweatshirt and lip balm are all good ideas—plus gloves (to protect your hands from rope burn) and a helmet, of course.

LEARNING to FLY

Your first time in the air should be in a tandem paraglider, alongside an experienced pilot instructor. During training, equipment is supplied by the club or flying school. (One reason for this is that few dealers will sell gear to a person without a rating.)

The essential steps of getting into the air are pretty simple. First, you lay your glider out, inspect it for wear and tear, and make sure that your lines aren't tangled. Your glider should be stretched out with the leading edge facing the direction you want to takeoff.

Next you have to strap into your harness. You'll want to take a couple of steps backward as you put on the harness, because once the front of your glider is off the ground, it will rise with the wind, which is a bad thing if you're not attached to it. Once strapped in, you're ready to take off.

You will normally launch your paraglider when there is a bit of a breeze. Moving forward and pulling your steering lines will let you inflate your canopy. Then you are ready to run, usually down the slope of a hill, into the wind. Unlike a hang glider which, because of its weight, requires you to commit to a launch once you get moving, a paraglider launch can be aborted just by slowing back down to a walk. Your glider will simply fall to the ground.

Once you get going, you'll accelerate to a sprint, and keep running until your feet leave the ground. Some instructors recommend that you keep pumping your legs until you are sure that you're rising as you may bump the ground a couple of times before you are clear. (It's the same reason planes don't raise their landing gear until they're at least a few hundred feet up.) On your first couple of flights, you'll likely just skim along the ground and come to rest at the bottom of the hill, but you can already sense the thrill of what it's like to soar like a bird. You'll also learn the basics of steering, which are pretty simple, really. Your control lines allow you to pull on the outside edges of your wing. This shifts the pendulum (you) slightly off center, which forces the edge of the glider to drop. This reduces airflow on the side you're pulling on and increases it on the opposite side, causing you to turn.

After you have mastered the basic take-off technique, you'll have an opportunity to really soar. The first stage is learning to recognize thermals, updrafts that are created as the earth warms during the day. Frequently they will be marked by the presence of soaring birds like hawks and buzzards, your new peers. As you get your glider over a thermal, the rising air will carry you with it. The record ceiling for a paraglider riding a thermal is more than 20,000 feet.

Once you reach a comfortable cruising altitude, you can make your way from thermal to thermal gently drifting downward as you move between them, only to be carried up in a slow gyre on the next column of warm air. You can also be carried aloft by "ridge lift," which is an updraft created by wind passing over a hill and being forced skyward as it crests a ridge. On an overcast day, this may be your best bet for getting into the sky.

Landing is much like takeoff. As you drift down you will want to face the wind and keep your legs relaxed. As you approach the ground, be ready to start running. When you first feel the ground, you can begin running on your toes, and then decelerate to a stop. You made it!

NEED TO KNOW

Like hang gliding, paragliding does not require a license but is a self-regulated sport under the auspices of the United States Hang Gliding Association (USHGA). Most local flying regulations require a pilot to have certain USHGA certified ratings, such as "Novice" or "Intermediate," before venturing out on an unsupervised flight. There are many places you can get your rating, but choose wisely. Make sure the instructors are certified by the USHGA.

PARAGLIDING PROS

Bob Drury didn't start out as a paraglider. He began with a successful career in rock climbing. After falling in love with the Himalayas on a climbing expedition in 1990, Drury took up paragliding and quickly made a name for himself. In 1997, he ventured back into the mountains he loved. With fellow British pilot John Silvester, he flew for a total of nearly 200 miles.

Drury returned to the Himalyas in 1998 with paragliders Robbie Whittall and Peter Brinkby. The trio reached altitudes of 23,000 feet. Drury is now known as a leader in his sport.

Whittall, a partner of Drury's, started out in hang gliding at age 16. He reached superstar status within two years, when he won the title "UK Champion" in the sport. One year after that, he became "World Champ." He switched to paragliding and, two years later, took home the gold at the paragliding world championships.

HANGING
WAY OUT

So you've had that flying dream again. The one in which you're soaring over the Rockies, watching the sun set before you, feeling the air rush past your arms and face, squinting toward the horizon as it turns pink and gold. The one where your slightest move sends you soaring in whatever direction you please. There's a way to make your dream come true.

Hang gliding is a death-defying sport that requires training and specialized equipment. It lacks some of the fly-or-die bravado of other sports, such as sky surfing, yet it allows the same kind of thrill for a much longer period of time. With a lightweight glider, harness, helmet, and precautionary parachute, you can become as airborne as a bird, taking flight for hours at a time. Most gliders find that once they've started, they're like homing pigeons—they always come back.

IT'S A BIRD,
IT'S A PLANE...

Hang gliding is a relatively new sport, but it definitely has a past. Modern hang gliding began with the constructions of Otto Lilienthal, a German aviator who built model wings with a makeshift harness and made about two thousand flights in the late 1800s. Shortly after him, the Wright brothers constructed hang gliders in the early 1900s in Kitty Hawk, North Carolina. The concept of hang gliding became all but extinct in the early 1900s with the emergence of the airplane itself. But after World War I, when Germany was prohibited from flying powered planes, the Germans instead used gliders, which could make flights of several hours over hundreds of miles.

Hang gliding returned in full force in the 1960s, thanks to the invention of an American engineer named Francis Rogallo. Using design plans for a kite, Rogallo created a pair of wings that were really a single piece of material joined at the center of the craft. The resulting delta shape was one of great interest to both aviators and NASA, which studied the design as a possible way for carrying its satellites back into the earth's atmosphere. Since Rogallo's design was simple and the materials cheap, pretty soon the general public had a chance to hang from wings and glide through the air.

The hang glider was further improved by the work of John Dickinson, an Australian engineer whose interests extended to water sports, including parasailing. Dickinson improved upon the triangle wing used to launch most parasailers, inventing a wing with a control bar, double harness, and central balance system. His model made it possible for a hang glider to weigh less than 45 pounds.

The first modern hang-glider manufacturer opened its doors in 1973. The Wills Wing company was the joint operation of Robert and Chris Wills, and is now the largest manufacturer of hang gliders in the United States. Many other manufacturers exist across the country as well, constructing gliders, helmets, parachutes, and harnesses.

HOW IT WORKS

A glider is an unpowered wing made of nylon or Mylar stretched over a rigid aluminum frame. The pilot is suspended from a strap connected to the glider, and controls its direction by shifting his weight.

Most hang gliders can climb to heights of 15,000 feet, just by riding air currents. They can pitch or roll with the slightest move and stay aloft for three hours or more.

The glider weighs from 45 to 70 pounds, but that weight is only shouldered at takeoff and landing.

To takeoff, hang gliders typically run down a hillside into the wind. It usually takes only a few strides—three or four—before liftoff. (Hang gliding does not require jumping off a cliff, although that is an option for the insane.) There is yet another way to launch called aero-towing. This method is considered the easiest way to learn to fly. The hang glider is on a platform and pulled behind a moving vehicle. At a high enough speed, the glider easily takes to the sky.

Once airborne, the challenge is to soar higher and higher. There are different ways to get there but the secret is in the air currents. Rising air comes in two forms: ridge lift and thermal lift. Ridge lift happens when horizontal wind hits an obstruction, such as a hill or a cliff, and is deflected upward. Pilots can climb by flying back and forth through the band of air. Thermal lift is air that rises as the sun heats the ground. (The same lift helps hot air balloons to rise.) Pilots simply circle the pocket of air, spiraling higher as they go. Thermal lift is enhanced near mountains, so hilly terrain is best for hang gliding.

Most people don't realize how cold it gets at higher altitudes. In fact, on a typical sunny day, the afternoon temperature will generally fall about five degrees Fahrenheit with every 1,000 feet of ascent. That means it might be 75 degrees on the ground and a chilly 60 at 3,000 feet. The bottom line is, even in summer the right wardrobe can make or break a comfortable ride.

LEARNING TO FLY

Aside from a glider and a little confidence, you'll need a slope in a clear area, which is steeper than six to one. You'll also need a little wind. Fifteen to 20 mph will do, but remember, when winds reach speeds higher than 30 mph, the ride starts to get a little bumpy.

Unlike aircraft pilots, hang gliding pilots are not required by law to be licensed. However, the United States Hang Gliding Association (USHGA) has worked out a deal with the Federal Aviation Administration. The two organizations agreed the hang gliding industry would remain self-regulated if the USHGA would institute a series of pilot proficiency ratings ("Beginner" through "Master"). Most flying sites require that pilots hold a USGHA rating before being allowed to fly.

You can earn your rating at most reputable hang gliding schools. Before choosing a school, find answers to these questions:

• What USHGA pilot ratings do the instructors have? ("Advanced Tandem Instructor" is the highest)
• What is the student-to-instructor ratio?
• Are flights radio supervised?
• Will training progress to higher hills?

• Does the school have hills to accommodate shifting wind directions, so flying is possible on most days?
• What is the school's safety record?
• How many students have been certified at the school?

Your first flight should be in tandem with an instructor. It will give you a taste of flying and get you primed for an introductory course. The formal course generally takes two days to complete and consists of solo flights under radio supervision. The idea is to progress to higher altitudes throughout the class. You also will learn the basics about launching, turning, and landing.

Learning to fly doesn't come easily to everyone, but most students can pick it up in five to 10 lessons, and are awarded one of the first two USHGA pilot ratings, "Beginner" or "Novice." Realistically, the process takes at least three months.

Hang gliding schools will supply a wing as part of the cost

of each course, so you won't have to shell out serious dough until after you've graduated. That's a good thing, because many dealers require a pilot rating before selling a glider to anyone.

Most gliders are designed to support between 90 and 250 pounds. When selecting your own, you'll want to get the help of your instructor. She'll know your strengths and weaknesses and can help guide you toward the right choice. She can also lend her expertise in evaluating what you're buying.

Other costs include a parachute and a helmet, plus you may also want to buy a two-way radio and a variometer, which tells you how high you've climbed and how fast you're going.

TIPS FROM AN AVID HANG GLIDER

Jayne DePanfilis is the executive director of the USHGA, and she has been hang gliding for three years.

What do you say to people who might be afraid to try hang gliding?

"There are a lot of misconceptions about the sport of hang gliding. Part of that fear comes from the fact that if man were meant to fly, we'd have wings. There's never been a better time to get into the sport of hang gliding. And the reason that there's never been a better time is because of the way the equipment has evolved, the certification process that the equipment goes through, the quality of instruction with certified instructors from the USHGA, and particularly the way the training methods have evolved."

Do you have any tips for beginners?

"Everyone learns at a different pace. You progress at your own pace; you progress at your own comfort level. Fly gliders that are below your skill level, in conditions that are below your skill level because the phrase is, 'It's better to be on the ground wishing you were in the air than be in the air wishing you were on the ground.'"

What's the best part of gliding?

"I think for people who've dreamed about flying, it's the total sense of freedom. It requires total concentration on what you're doing. If you had a bad day at the office, you forget about all of it because you're flying. And you're free. And when you're flying, no one can tell you what to do."

BEST SONGS TO LISTEN TO WHILE HANG GLIDING

"Gliding By" – Joyce Cooling

"Hang On Now" – Kajagoogoo

"Blowin' in the Wind" – Bob Dylan

"Hangin' Tough" – New Kids on the Block

"Superglider" – Drugstore Montiero

"Clouds at My Feet" – Locust

"Hang Glider" – Bonnie Pink

"Flying Not Falling" – Graham Bonnet

"Gracefully Gliding" – Janice Robinson

"Into the Great Wide Open" – Tom Petty and The Heartbreakers

4
SPLASH
ATTACK

We've covered some of the "fun" on land and in the air, so now it's time to look at how you can tempt fate in your favorite body of water (unless you take a swim through the Manhattan stretch of the Hudson River, in which case, you've already tempted fate).

Whether you prefer the rolling surf of the clear blue ocean, a glassy lake perfect for making your own waves, or a river that erupts like a whitewater volcano as you're trying to shoot downstream, this chapter has something for you.

From staples such as surfing and Xtreme water skiing, to whitewater rafting and kayaking, to budding sports like wakeboarding, keep reading and find out why the pull of the current is so strong for water lovers.

SURF'S UP

HANG TIME

Modern surfing's roots run deep through the lush, tropical islands of the Pacific Ocean. It's believed that ancient Polynesians first hit the waves with specially carved wooden canoes, and later, Hawaiians—royalty in particular—developed what we know today as the sport of surfing. But despite all the changes in equipment, style, and attitude, the essence of surfing has remained intact. No matter how you carve it, the soul of surfing is *all* about the ride.

CAUTION FIRST

Prior to charging the waves, you need to understand the power of the ocean, your own physical limits, and how to evaluate the two together. Warning: Even though surfing is statistically a safe sport, many people have lost their lives by being careless. The mix of tides, rip currents, backwashes, and big swells can be a dangerous cocktail, overpowering even the strongest of swimmers. Don't let this scare you off. Just be mindful of what the ocean can do and know your limitations.

You should feel confident in your swimming abilities before catching your first wave. There will be times when you lose your board 50 yards or more away from the beach and have to swim into shore to recover it. You don't want to have to be rescued by the lifeguard, do you? (Unless it's one of those *Baywatch* people.) You will never be able to show your face on that beach again.

Also, always be mindful of rip currents when surfing. These "rivers" are formed when waves push water in toward the beach. It eventually needs to get back out to sea, so it tends to funnel together and shoot out in a powerful stream. The bigger the waves, the more water that is driven toward the beach, and the stronger the rip currents that go back out. Rips churn up the bottom and appear murky in color, almost like chocolate milk. If you get caught in a rip, do not fight it. Not even that big Australian Olympic swimmer, the Thorpedo, can power though a strong rip tide. Use your head instead: Stroke out of the rip, swimming parallel to the coast, until you are out of the stream. Then head toward the beach.

The World of Waves

In the most general sense, waves are formed by wind. While there may be other factors—like landslides, earthquakes, or alien spaceships crashing into the ocean—the rule of thumb is: The stronger the wind and the longer it blows on the surface of the ocean, the larger the waves will be. That's the basic theory. While wind generates waves, the contour of the ocean floor is what causes them to break in all sizes and shapes. Here are the three main types of breaks.

Beach Breaks

Waves here break onto a sandy bottom. Most often this causes waves to roll in a softer, wheeling style, usually the best choice for beginners. But be on your guard. Just because there is sand down there doesn't mean it's safe. Some beach breaks are notorious for creating gnarly waves.

Reef or Rock Breaks

Simply stated, a reef break is where waves break over a submerged reef or rock formation. Often shallow and dangerous, these setups can create dramatic barreling waves that are suited only for experts—or beginners looking for a thrashing.

Point Breaks

Point break waves wrap around and break where a piece of land juts out into the ocean. This type of spot is usually very consistent; it creates uniform waves, and can make for long rides.

CHOOSE YOUR WEAPON

The surfboard a rider chooses is like the sword selected by a samurai warrior. The right choice could mean the difference between winning or losing. Surfers today ride anything from ultra-light, high-performance shortboards (often called potato chips because of their scrawny size) to the old-school longboards from the original Beach Boys' days. And in between the two extremes is a wide array of choices. You can ride a fish, a thruster, a slug, an egg, a fun board, and even something called a rhino chaser (designed specifically for massive waves that would injure mere mortals like us). When first starting out, your best chance to shorten the learning curve is to pick up a big, wide longboard from the local shop. The wider a board is, the more forgiveness it offers inexperienced riders. These bigger boards are also easier to paddle. Hold off on a new smaller stick (the cool term for surfboard) until you're confident in your skills

or aching to launch five foot airs. Before you leave the shop, also pick up some wax, for traction on the board, and a leash. The leash attaches you to your board and saves you lots of swimming.

LANDLUBBERS

So, you now know what to look for before you get in the water. And you have picked a nice big board to start. Now you need to work on what to do before you get on that giant piece of foam and fiberglass. Think of this as the "training wheel" stage.

In the comfort of your own home (because this could be highly embarrassing if done in public), work on the most crucial step in surfing—the pop-up. Just lie down prone on your floor and press your hands to the ground as if you were doing a push-up. Quickly raise your torso up and, at the same time, swing your knees and lower body underneath you. The goal is to land with your feet pointed to one side and beneath your shoulders. Your knees should be bent, and your upper body relaxed. In the

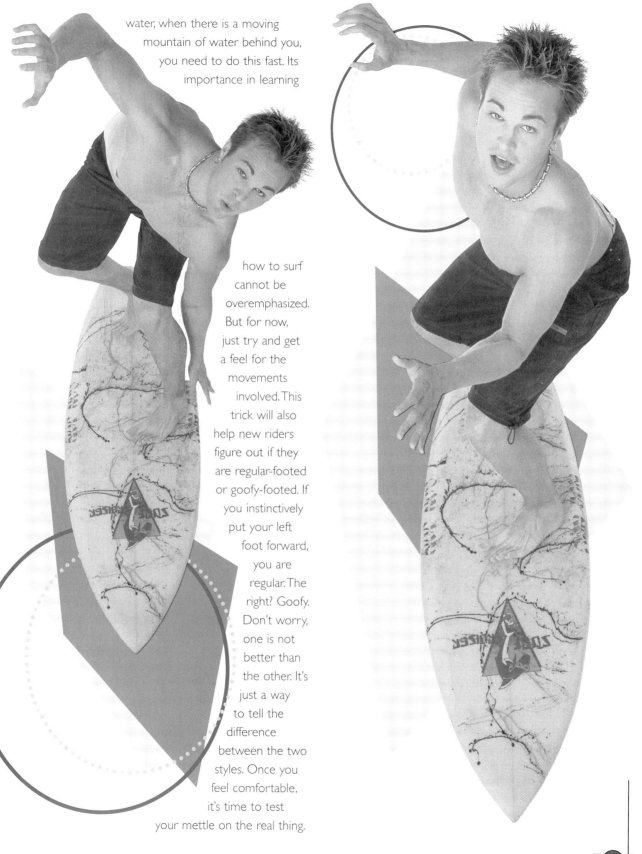

water, when there is a moving mountain of water behind you, you need to do this fast. Its importance in learning how to surf cannot be overemphasized. But for now, just try and get a feel for the movements involved. This trick will also help new riders figure out if they are regular-footed or goofy-footed. If you instinctively put your left foot forward, you are regular. The right? Goofy. Don't worry, one is not better than the other. It's just a way to tell the difference between the two styles. Once you feel comfortable, it's time to test your mettle on the real thing.

GETTING WET

It's time. You have your board waxed and under your arm. You attached your leash to your back foot (remember, regular and goofy?), and your surf trunks are double-knotted. This last point is important. Naked surfing is highly overrated. Before hanging ten, step back

and take five. Look out at the water and see what is happening. How are the waves

breaking? Where is the lineup (the place where surfers line up to catch waves)? Are the waves coming to shore in sets? If you take a few minutes to scope the scene, you'll save yourself time and effort, and score plenty of waves. Surfing is not just a physical activity. You do need to use your brain.

While you are checking the break, stretch out the muscles you'll be using most, starting with your arms. You do 10 times more paddling than actual standing. Next, stretch

out your legs and your back. Finally, it's time to surf. But wait, did you remember the sunscreen? Skin cancer will put a real damper on your surfing career. Always toss on some lotion of SPF 15 or higher. You'll thank us later. But stay away from the neon stuff. It is very not cool.

As you wade out into the water, keep the nose of your board pointed toward the surf. If it turns sideways, you're likely to get clobbered if a wave catches the board. That wouldn't be a great start. When you're about waist deep, lay on your board and work on finding a balance point. This will feel awkward at first, like trying to lie on top of a huge seesaw. When you get comfortable, start to paddle, again always keeping the nose of the board pointed at the waves.

This is just like swimming the freestyle stroke, only easier. When your hand is in the water, pull deliberately, don't just splash around. This should get you moving. But don't go too far.

STARTING SMALL

The best place to learn surfing fundamentals is in the white water—the foamy section created after a wave crumbles. It's easier to start here because the waves don't have as much juice as they do when they initially break. It's like learning to drive in a parking lot and not on the busy interstate. To get started, spin the board around so the nose is facing the beach and stand off on the side like you're a cowboy ready to mount a horse. As a wave nears, jump

onto your board, making sure you have some forward momentum. Your timing may need some work on the first few attempts, but the ultimate plan is for the wave's energy to pick you and the board up and carry you toward the beach. When you feel the power of the swell pushing you, all you have to do is stand up. Easy, right? Just remember back to your training session and the fine art of popping up. Now is your chance to shine.

THE **REAL DEAL**

After you have conquered the inside white water area (and it's not likely that this will happen quickly; surfing takes lots of practice), it's time to leave the parking lot and head out on the big road. Just getting out to the lineup can take some work. You'll need to learn the art of negotiating incoming waves to better enjoy this sport. When the waves are small, it's possible just to paddle right over the top of incoming swells. But this is rare. Usually you'll need a plan of attack. There

are two methods for taking on waves as you head out: the turtle roll and the duck dive. The turtle roll, or just the roll, is designed primarily for longboards. Here's the skinny: As the white water approaches, a rider grabs the two rails (a fancy name for the sides of the board) firmly, rolls the board upside down, and waits as the wave passes over top. It's important to glue-grip the board when the foamy section hits you. Hold on to that baby as tight as you can, losing your board ranks right up there with trunk rash.

As a beginner, you won't need the duck dive because it's nearly impossible to perform on a longboard. But the idea is for a rider to press his weight down on the front of the board, kneel on the back, and sink the stick as a wave shoots over top of him. When the breaker has passed, you spring up behind, unscathed, and continue paddling.

Once in the lineup, keep in mind the unwritten but very strict rules of surfing. In the past 10 years, surfing's popularity has skyrocketed, but the number of surf spots has not. The first rule, and the one that is most often broken by beginners, is: one wave, one rider. End

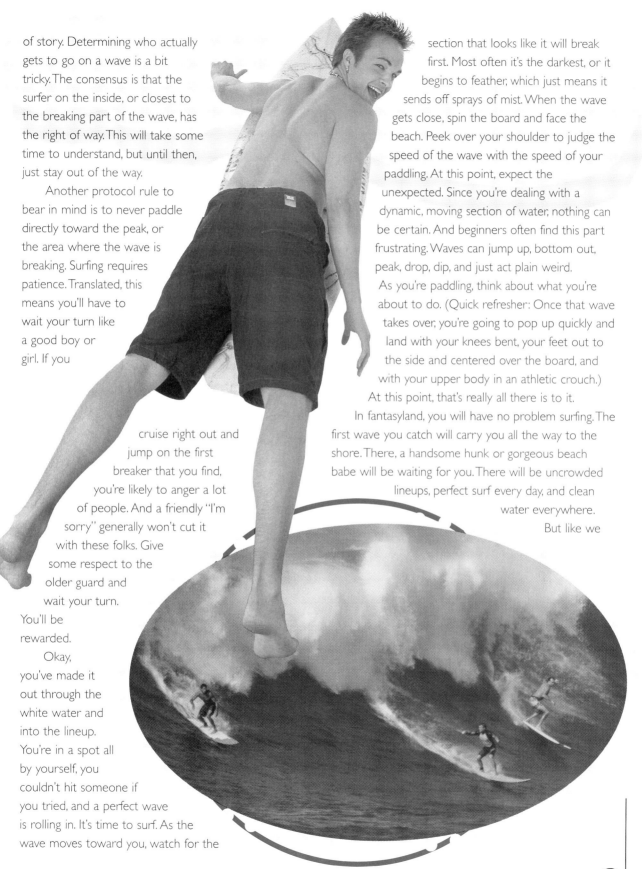

of story. Determining who actually gets to go on a wave is a bit tricky. The consensus is that the surfer on the inside, or closest to the breaking part of the wave, has the right of way. This will take some time to understand, but until then, just stay out of the way.

Another protocol rule to bear in mind is to never paddle directly toward the peak, or the area where the wave is breaking. Surfing requires patience. Translated, this means you'll have to wait your turn like a good boy or girl. If you cruise right out and jump on the first breaker that you find, you're likely to anger a lot of people. And a friendly "I'm sorry" generally won't cut it with these folks. Give some respect to the older guard and wait your turn. You'll be rewarded.

Okay, you've made it out through the white water and into the lineup. You're in a spot all by yourself, you couldn't hit someone if you tried, and a perfect wave is rolling in. It's time to surf. As the wave moves toward you, watch for the section that looks like it will break first. Most often it's the darkest, or it begins to feather, which just means it sends off sprays of mist. When the wave gets close, spin the board and face the beach. Peek over your shoulder to judge the speed of the wave with the speed of your paddling. At this point, expect the unexpected. Since you're dealing with a dynamic, moving section of water, nothing can be certain. And beginners often find this part frustrating. Waves can jump up, bottom out, peak, drop, dip, and just act plain weird.

As you're paddling, think about what you're about to do. (Quick refresher: Once that wave takes over, you're going to pop up quickly and land with your knees bent, your feet out to the side and centered over the board, and with your upper body in an athletic crouch.) At this point, that's really all there is to it.

In fantasyland, you will have no problem surfing. The first wave you catch will carry you all the way to the shore. There, a handsome hunk or gorgeous beach babe will be waiting for you. There will be uncrowded lineups, perfect surf every day, and clean water everywhere. But like we

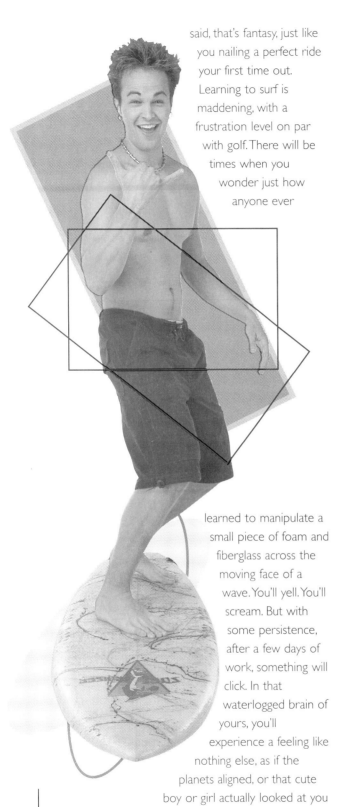

said, that's fantasy, just like you nailing a perfect ride your first time out. Learning to surf is maddening, with a frustration level on par with golf. There will be times when you wonder just how anyone ever learned to manipulate a small piece of foam and fiberglass across the moving face of a wave. You'll yell. You'll scream. But with some persistence, after a few days of work, something will click. In that waterlogged brain of yours, you'll experience a feeling like nothing else, as if the planets aligned, or that cute boy or girl actually looked at you and smiled, but it's ten times better. You'll be surfing. And it's a great feeling.

MOVING UP

The thrill of riding straight toward the beach will last for a few hours, but eventually as a surfer (which you now can officially call yourself), you'll want to get the most out of every wave. The first step will be to start angling across a wave, or what riders generally call going "on the line." This requires reading a wave a bit more. Since waves are not straight, often they will peel, or break, not all at once but rather in a continuous line.

With some experience (you can't really teach this), surfers learn to scan a breaker as it nears the beach and to tell in which direction it will peel. They then position themselves on an angle to shoot down the

line, across the face of the wave. This technique allows riders to gain tremendous amounts of speed, and in turn lets them rip some huge maneuvers. Plus it's much more fun.

The first turn (bottom turn) is crucial. Put simply, it's the initial turn a rider makes after popping up, dropping in, and shooting down the face of the wave. The bottom turn lets riders get into position to trim on a wave, so its execution is crucial for everything that will come later in the ride.

A good bottom turn is ballet on a board. It is graceful, effortless, and efficient. Yours may not fit these descriptions off the bat, but you will someday. The key to a good bottom turn is timing; you need to know where and when to do it. But that will come with practice. For now it's a matter of nailing the basics.

After you slide down the front of the wave, if your toes are pointing toward the face (called riding frontside), you'll want to put moderate pressure on your toes and the balls of your feet. You'll also need to have your weight resting slightly on your back foot. If your back and heels are to the wave (riding backside), you'll want to put the pressure on your heels, with more weight falling on the back foot. Swing your hips and shoulders to get better movement out of your turns. With practice you'll realize that different combinations of foot placement, weight distribution, and upper body movement can drastically affect all your moves.

SUPERstar

Once you have perfected your bottom turn and you can successfully angle across a wave, the only thing stopping you from becoming the next Kelly Slater is your own innovation and determination. And the only way you're

going to get better is to get in the water and surf. It's as simple as that. So hit the waves already.

LONG LIVE THE KING

Few personalities have done more for the sport of surfing than Kelly Slater. He assaulted the sport with an arsenal of new tricks on parts of the waves never before imagined, and a tube-riding talent that routinely dropped jaws along any beach he surfed. He brought a new way to look at wave riding that captivated crunchy old-timers, his peers, and the growing fans of the sport alike. In return for his progressive and visionary approach to the timeless sport, he earned an unprecedented six World Titles, became the most popular surfer to ever stand on a board, and earned a place atop the sport he has loved since childhood.

Slater emerged from wave-starved Cocoa Beach, Florida—an unlikely breeding ground for the man who would become surfing's undisputed king. Surfing was a way of life for the Slater family. He was on the road at an early age, traveling throughout California and Hawaii, being raised on the roots of surfing. All of it was training for his arrival on the professional tour. But experience alone would not take Slater far. Luckily, he had god-given talent.

In surfboard shaper Al Merrick's words, "Kelly has an uncanny knowledge of his body's movement and location in time and space." It wasn't long before Slater was capitalizing on this talent, not only winning, but demolishing the competitive scene. Steve Hawk, former editor of *Surfer Magazine*, said that, "Kelly has all of the physical gifts-—balance, reflexes, strength. He can just see and react so quickly." Many, though, attribute Slater's success to his drive. Added Hawk, "Slater loves a challenge. He thrives on it." His record supports that.

In 1995, Slater entered the Pipeline Masters competition ranked third in the world. Few considered him a real threat to take the title, but Slater swept through the event like a rhino in full charge, surfing what many long-time observers claim is the best heat ever in the semi-final against friend and fellow pro Rob Machado. Slater again stood atop the winner's podium.

Aside from re-writing the record books, Slater is credited with leading the new approach to high performance surfing that dominates the sport today. From the moment they arrived, like the restless hotshots they were, Slater and his younger peers were challenging the older guard and the traditional way surfing was approached. Borrowing from the skateboarding and snowboarding worlds, the young, cavalier New School crowd was blowing minds with moves only dreamed of: Aerials, tailslides, and indy grabs were part of many a surfer's regular routine. Slater was the point man for the whole revolution.

Today, Slater has almost outgrown the dimensions of the global sport. To many, he embodies surfing. He has become an international ambassador, his popularity not confined to beach bums lounging on the coast. Kids from Bozeman, Montana, to Berlin, Germany, some of whom have never seen the ocean, know who Kelly Slater is. He has never lost his love for the sport.

In 2000, Slater announced he was taking some time off from the relentless world of professional surfing. Some in the sport questioned if he was losing his motivation. They wondered if his drive and love for riding waves was gone. But in the time since his decision, it's become clear that he is perhaps more in love with the sport than ever. He travels around the world now not because he has to, but because he is returning to the roots of the sport. He is surfing not for the fame, nor for the money. He has all that. Slater is surfing for the love. He is surfing just to surf.

WITH THE WIND

If you sit alone in the dark, cursing your lack of a boat or access to one, knowing that water skiing and wakeboarding are out of the question, and asking what is there to look forward to except the next episode of *Jackass*, there is an answer. It's one of the most accessible and athletic ways to get wet and wild: Wind surfing, which is also called boardsailing because of some weird trademark thing held by the people who manufactured the first wind surf board. If visions of easy riding in on the waves enters your mind, quickly whisk them away; wind surfing is an Xtreme sport that makes some serious athletic demands.

With wind surfing, you don't have to launch from a boat dock, so just about any body of water will work; you can transport the equipment to and from your destination in even the smallest car (with the help of a roof rack); and wind surfing will keep you in great shape. Also, the more wind the better—with boat sports such as water skiing and wakeboarding, when the wind picks up, the boats usually head in. The big waves were made for "board-heads."

THE LONG AND THE SHORT OF IT

While the tools of the trade can get pretty complicated, the basics are simple. For a beginner, the wind surfing equipment you need is fairly

straightforward. Let's start with the board. There are three main types: long boards, mid-length boards, and short boards. Aside from the length (the factor in primary consideration here), all boards are technically the same. They have a foam core with the outer layer either made of polypropylene or fiberglass. A fiberglass board will be a little lighter, but is easier to damage. The poly boards are the best bet when starting out because, even though they are a little heavier, they can stand up to the beating they are subjected to by a clumsy beginner. (That's you.)

As for length, short boards are used in stronger winds. Because they are more difficult to control and balance, short boards are for experienced wind surfers only. Don't worry; it doesn't take too long to graduate to that category with a little practice. You should also know when you run out to get yourself a board, a short board is typically 325 cm

beginners and offers experts an easy ride. Long boards usually measure 350 cm (just over 11' 4") or more and have more buoyancy than the shorter boards. These qualities make a long board more stable and allow it to be used in a variety of wind conditions. Also, when you choose your long board (or any board), keep in mind how much you weigh. Any reputable surf shop will give you a good range.

THE RIG

Most beginner boards come packaged with a rig: the sail, mast, and boom. You will probably want to get a sail between 18 to 21 square feet. This size will handle most of the wind conditions you will face as a beginner and intermediate wind surfer. When you first enter the world of wind surfing, you will want to familiarize yourself with the sail terminology (and there's plenty of it) like battens, tack, clew, and downhaul.

Bill Doster/Wind Surfing Magazine

(10' 6") or smaller.

Mid-length boards are not as difficult for a beginner to control, but they are not as stable as long boards. A mid-length board is more versatile, offering a good in-between option when you want to take that next step up the wind surfing mast.

Now for the long board, the one that welcomes

Bill Doster/Wind Surfing Magazine

The main terms you need to know are simple. The mast is a long rod. It slides inside the front of the sail (aka the luff) into the luff tube. While you are shopping for your newest toy, check out the availability of two-piece masts—they are much easier to transport. Also take a look at the price. If you were to buy just the mast, you would discover it is not a cheap piece of equipment. Keep in mind, though, that it is specially designed to be lightweight and very strong. It is also stiff, but can give when put under extreme pressure. This isn't the type of thing you can substitute with the pole that holds up your volleyball net.

Boom shaka-laka—yep, next comes the boom. This is what you hold on to when you are mastering the sport of wind surfing. It is slightly bow-shaped, most are adjustable in length, and it has been designed to clamp to the mast to allow for height adjustment.

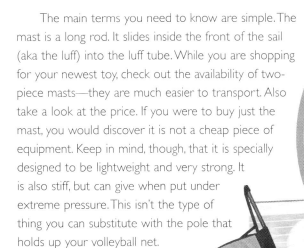

ACCESSORIZE!

Because wind surfing is a sport in which, duh, the wind blows, you might want to consider investing in a wetsuit. When the temperatures are chilly, and the wind and water are calling your name, you'll be glad you have one.

As mentioned earlier, it helps to have a roof rack to transport your equipment, especially if you have a vehicle that won't accommodate a board, sail, and mast—or in other words, most cars.

WIND SURFING 101

As the wind and the waves beckon you, there are a few more things you should know, such as how to get your board positioned on the water. To do this, you use

Todd Mehling/Wind Surfing Magazine

a method called uphauling. A key to getting this right is trying it first *out* of deep water. Yep, before you hit the waves, hit the shallow water at the beach. While standing on the board with your feet on either side of the mast, bend your knees and grab close to the mast base and pull the sail out of the water slowly, allowing the water to run off the sail. Once it's up and you are standing with your knees bent, grab the mast with both hands below the boom. Now, release the back hand and twist your body to face forward. The back foot will slide back as the front foot pivots to face forward.

Once the rig has been pulled in slightly and feels balanced, you can grab the boom with the back hand. When comfortable, in other words when you feel totally balanced and with both hands on the boom, the sail will begin to fill with air for the first time, and you will feel a pull against your body, so adjust the bend of your knees to help control your balance.

BALANCING ACT

Once you are up, the first thing you need to master is balance. After you've got that down, you can practice powering the sail. This is where the wind comes in. Experiment with how the rig moves and how it responds to the wind direction. If you ever feel like you are losing your balance, you should loosen or let go with your back hand. As you get to know the rig, you will figure out how to steer and to change direction. One maneuver, called the jibe, is very handy if you don't want to head on a one-way trip to Japan. When you start to lose momentum from the wind, whip the mast around and move to the opposite side of the board. You can also duck under the mast. If the board is now moving in the opposite direction, and you're not swimming, then you did it. All it takes is a little practice. Believe it or not, that is the extent of the beginner skills. Once you get them down, you can call yourself an intermediate wind surfer. At least out of ear shot of the best board-heads.

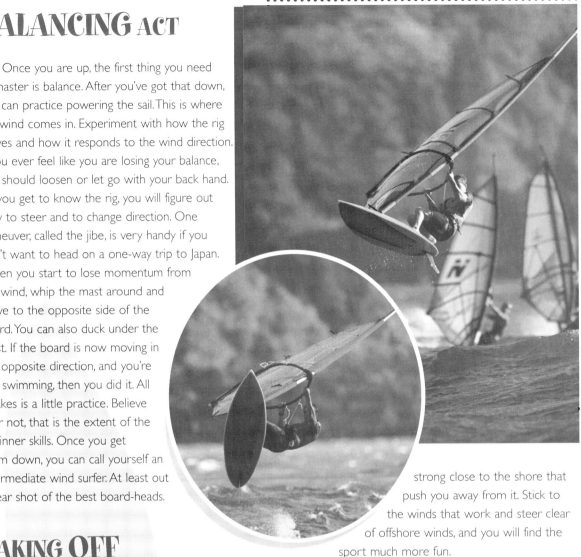

TAKING OFF

After you master the basics, it's time to move on to deeper waters. At the top of the sport, you will be facing large waves and strong winds, experiencing the thrill of taking to the air with jumps, and mastering one trick after another. Since the essence of wind surfing is taking advantage of the wind, it's nice to know a little bit about what you are dealing with. There are three wind directions: sideshore (ideal), onshore (usually good), and offshore (very bad). Sideshore wind blows across the launch area (meaning right to left or vice versa), onshore winds blow so that you can mainly move in a line parallel to the shore rather than to and from, and offshore winds are those ones that are really strong close to the shore that push you away from it. Stick to the winds that work and steer clear of offshore winds, and you will find the sport much more fun.

When it comes to getting the most out of what you have invested in wind surfing in terms of equipment, the bottom line is the time you are willing to invest. Each hour you spend on the water will improve how you jibe (turn the board away from the wind), how you handle strong winds, and how well you make your equipment work for you. You'll splash into the water a few times, but just swim back to your board and pick up the wind again. Make the most of the sport. Get on the board with someone else (try that one on a surfboard—and be sure you record it so your friends can laugh at you later), or experiment with different types of sails. There are so many things to try, so get started.

WAKE UP

THE BOARD NECESSITIES

The initial key to wakeboarding success is finding the right board. First, never buy until you try. You don't want to invest in a shiny new wakeboard until you know it is the right one for you, and the only way to know is to take it out for a ride. Some surf shops have test days when they allow prospective customers to try out their merchandise. If this is not an option where you live, try renting a few

Maybe you've seen a wakeboarder in action on ESPN or while catching a few rays at the beach or lake. Did it look like a surfer was being pulled like a water skier on an object that resembled an overweight snowboard? That's pretty much what it is. You're basically being puled along, and launching into the air off the boat's wake (and hopefully doing some fancy moves while airborne).

Wakeboarding was born in the 1980s when an inventive San Diego surfer, Tony Finn, decided to combine surfing and water skiing into one sport. His first board was a small surfboard to which he eventually attached foot straps. This design became the Skurfer. Because the Skurfer was difficult to get up on and had limited stability, Herb O'Brien, the owner of H.O. Sports, began modifying and experimenting with the boards. In the early 1990s, his efforts resulted in the first "wakeboard," the Hyperlite.

With equipment continually refined, wakeboarding has become an extreme action sport that's also fairly easy to learn, so that moving from the beginner to intermediate category doesn't take long (a plus for those who tend toward negative attention spans). Wakeboarding also lends itself to tricks, which is one of its main appeals.

different boards to test them out.

Obviously you need to know what to look for in the board itself. Start with the length and width. Longer boards can support more weight, so check the maximum weight recommendation provided by most board manufacturers. Although a shorter board may seem to turn faster and easier, it's better to have your board on the long side. As for width, the rounder the board, the slower it will go, but a board that is too narrow can cause stability problems. Try out a few different boards, and keep in mind that the first few rides on any unfamiliar wakeboard will be shaky.

The curve of the board is also a feature you want to consider. The wakeboard shouldn't be flat; each end of the board should have a gradual upward curve, and these vary from board to board. You just have to experiment to find what works best for you.

When browsing through rows of wakeboards begging you to strap them on, do not forget about the fins. Imagine a fish without fins; that's you on a wakeboard, because fins play a large part in how the board rides and maneuvers. Larger fins provide more carve and a more stable ride, while smaller fins allow faster, quicker movement. The number of fins is also a factor. There can be one, two, or three fins at each end of a board, so don't even think about slapping down a few Benjamins without comparing the feel of the fins on the water.

Once Striker (or whatever endearing name you've given your wakeboard) is tucked safely in the boat, pull out the rope. If it is a non-adjustable rope intended for water skiing, head back to the dock. You want a rope with sections that can be removed to adjust the length of the rope. The rope is measured sort of backwards, not by how long it is but by how much you take off. A standard rope is 75-feet, which could be adjusted to 15 feet off (making it 60 feet), 22 feet off, 28 feet off, etc. A beginner would usually start around 32 feet off. A shorter rope keeps the boarder closer to the boat and makes it easier to cross the wakes and learn beginner jumps. As skill levels increase, a longer rope allows more freedom, bigger moves, and more air time.

THE NITTY GRITTY

Nope, you still aren't ready to start skimming the water. A few other things you might want to consider are the length of your pylon (the pole or the back of the boat where the rope attaches), having the boat going the right speed for the sport, and knowing the language. Every sport has its own terminology; to be a pro (or sound like one) you better be able to talk the talk as well as spin the spin.

Whether you need a ski pylon is not even a question when wakeboarding; it is a must. The question is: Should you invest in a pylon extension? Generally speaking, yes. With a normal pylon, the rope ends up angling and pulling down, which limits the amount of air you can achieve. A pylon extension pulls the rope's angle upward, which gives you more time to perform each

move, buys more air time, and gives you the chance to perfect a soft landing.

As for boat speed, stick to no less than 15 mph and no more than 18 mph when starting out. As you improve, you can give the driver thumbs up to increase the speed, but you will probably stick to speeds under 25 mph. Anything faster and all you will be doing is trying to keep from tanking.

Now about talking the talk. This isn't about knowing to yell "hit it" when you are ready for the boat to pull you up or knowing what a pylon is. If you do know what a spin and a roll are, you are on your way. You can't claim to be an expert just because you can do the moves; you have to also know what to call them. From a Backside 360 Heli Hand Pass to a Tantrum-to-fakie, there is a lot to be learned. You should also familiarize yourself with the boat, wake, and air lingo, like what it means to "Double Up" and how to get "Phatter" wakes. Start watching those wakeboarding competitions. Pay attention to what the announcers say; you might also want to watch what the boarders are doing since it doesn't matter that you know there is a move called the Switchstance Backside Roll if you have no idea what it looks like.

UP AND AT IT

Now that you're more familiar with the lingo of wakeboarding, it's time to take the plunge. Toss your board in the water and then jump in after it (try not to land on it though, so you don't end up injured *before* you even get up). Then, strap those bindings on your feet. If getting the bindings on seems difficult, you might want to bring a little dish soap along next time. Remember *dish soap,*

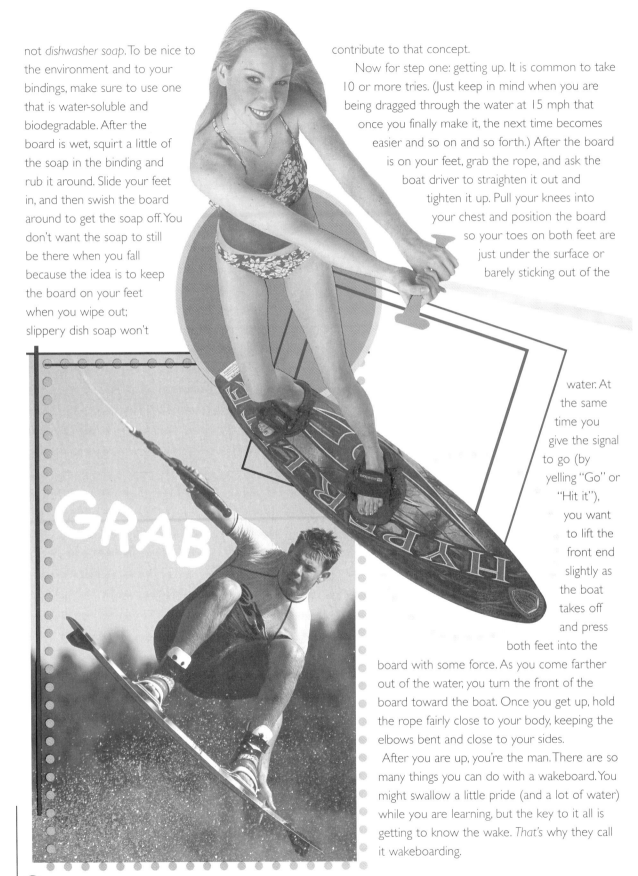

not *dishwasher soap*. To be nice to the environment and to your bindings, make sure to use one that is water-soluble and biodegradable. After the board is wet, squirt a little of the soap in the binding and rub it around. Slide your feet in, and then swish the board around to get the soap off. You don't want the soap to still be there when you fall because the idea is to keep the board on your feet when you wipe out; slippery dish soap won't

contribute to that concept.

Now for step one: getting up. It is common to take 10 or more tries. (Just keep in mind when you are being dragged through the water at 15 mph that once you finally make it, the next time becomes easier and so on and so forth.) After the board is on your feet, grab the rope, and ask the boat driver to straighten it out and tighten it up. Pull your knees into your chest and position the board so your toes on both feet are just under the surface or barely sticking out of the water. At the same time you give the signal to go (by yelling "Go" or "Hit it"), you want to lift the front end slightly as the boat takes off and press both feet into the board with some force. As you come farther out of the water, you turn the front of the board toward the boat. Once you get up, hold the rope fairly close to your body, keeping the elbows bent and close to your sides.

After you are up, you're the man. There are so many things you can do with a wakeboard. You might swallow a little pride (and a lot of water) while you are learning, but the key to it all is getting to know the wake. *That's* why they call it wakeboarding.

GRAB

BUST a MOVE!

Just to get your feet wet, so to speak, here are a few definitions:

SPIN

A maneuver in which a wakeboarder changes his position relative to the boat, in a horizontal plane. In simpler terms, spins involve turning around, and usually require changing your grip on the rope. In a backside 360, for instance, the wakeboarder begins by facing the boat, with both hands gripping the handle of the rope. Then he releases the rope with one hand, catches air, pulls the rope behind his back, spins in the direction of the free hand until his back is to the boat, shifts his grip on the rope from one hand to the other, and returns to the forward-facing position with both hands gripping the handle, as he re-connects with the water, knees deeply bent.

INVERT

As in skateboarding and in-line skating, inverts involve getting airborne and throwing one's feet (and thus one's wakeboard) into a position that is perpendicular to the surface of the water. In most cases, the board (and rider) will literally be inverted, or upside down, for a moment. Various versions of Mobes, tantrums, flips, and rolls are all varieties of inverts. Some specific inverts include the Front Roll, the Indy Glide, the Tootsie Roll, the Moby Dick, and the Indy Tantrum.

GRAB

This refers to reaching down with a free hand and gripping the surface of the board, while airborne. Each spot on the board sports its own nickname. A tail grab, for instance, obviously involves gripping the rear of the board, while a nose grab refers to grabbing the front of the board. Less obvious terms for grabs include Indy (middle of the board, between the feet, in front of you), Stalefish (middle of the board, between the feet, behind you), and Crail (gripping the area in front of the left foot with the right hand).

WAKESKATE

Refers to a modified board that is considerably narrower than a wakeboard. It resembles a standard water ski with either end chopped off, but has no bindings. Much like a skateboarder, a wakeskater is free to shift his feet on the surface of the board, or even to lift his feet temporarily. Because nothing but gravity and elastic soles hold a rider on the board, wakeskating is especially challenging. Previous mastery of skateboarding moves is a distinct advantage when attempting this sport.

GETTING STARTED: SOME TRICKS AND HOW TO DO THEM

Surfing the wake: Once you've mastered getting up, the next step is to surf the wake. By learning to surf comfortably you'll lay the foundation for all subsequent tricks and moves you want to tackle.

Move about ten feet outside the wake, knees bent, toes pointing toward the wake. Gradually apply enough pressure with your toes to begin sliding toward the wake. When you get to within about three feet of the wake, shift your weight to your heels. This should cause you to bank off the rise of the wake and cruise back out to your starting position. Experiment with different degrees of heel pressure. By tilting the board sharply you should eventually be able to kick up a fan of water with your heelside.

Butter Slide: Begin as you would for surfing. From about ten feet out, approach the wake with sufficient speed to get you to the lip of the wake. Crest the peak and apply pressure with your heels as you bring the handle to the middle of your hips. As your back fin breaks free, keep equal pressure on your heels, keep your knees bent and use the rope's tension to maintain your balance. You should now be riding the crest of the wake, with your board perpendicular to the boat. Avoid putting any pressure on your toes while butter sliding, or you will tumble forward. To return to your starting position, apply extra pressure to the heel of your back foot and pull the handle to your front hip. Practice repeatedly.

Ollie 180: This will be your first aerial maneuver. Begin by moving about 15 feet outside the wake. Experiment first with a simple bunny hop ollie. Press down on your rear foot while lifting with your front foot and push off with both knees. This will raise the front of your board out of the water. Now you're ready to fly. Repeat the above maneuver. After lifting your front foot, raise your back foot as well. This will send you sailing momentarily. Practice repeatedly until you're comfortable, attempting to increase your lift to about one foot above the water. Allow your forward hand to float free; it may be extended for balance. To introduce the 180, do the ollie. While airborne, pull the handle with your back hand to your back hip. This will rotate your body in midair, so that you're perpendicular to the boat. Continue swinging around until your back foot is in the lead foot position. Shifting your weight slightly to your back foot, and keeping the handle low, make your perfect landing.

LOOK, MA, NO SKIS!

Barefoot skiing, or barefooting, is the toughest kind of waterskiing there is. You plane across the water at minimum speeds of 30 miles per hour, with the soles of your feet subbing for water skis. It can happen to you—of course, it helps to know how to ski with real skis first.

SKIING BACKWASH

Waterskiing was invented in the United States in 1922, when Ralph Samuelson tested the first pair of skis on water. The sport quickly caught on in the 1920s and early 1930s and officially developed into a competitive sport in 1939, with the formation of the American Water Ski Association. It was the AWSA (now known as USA Water Ski) that sanctioned the first annual National Water Ski Championships at Jones Beach on Long Island, New York.

Today, USA Water Ski oversees organized waterskiing in the United States and is responsible for certifying instructors of the sport. As a recreational waterskier you won't need to be licensed, but getting comfortable with the sport takes a little time.

People first started going ski-less in Florida during the late 1940s. Barefooting quickly caught on and was introduced into waterski shows. In 1961, USA Water Ski organized the American Barefoot Club (ABC) for barefooters who could stay on their feet for a minimum of 60 seconds. The barefoot craze became especially big in Australia, and it was the Australians who eventually organized the first tournaments.

Today, barefooting is a worldwide sport recognized by the International Water Ski Federation. A world championship competition is held every two years. In most contests, barefooters must show their stuff in wake slalom, tricks, and jumping.

Doug Dukane/Water Ski Magazine

REGULAR SKIING:
THE 9-STEP PROGRAM

1 Place the skis snuggly on your feet.

2 Put the rope between your knees and the handle in your hands.

3 Your knees should be bent toward your chest.

4 Your skis will be shoulder-length apart, pointing toward the boat, with between six and 12 inches of ski above the water's surface.

5 Once the boat starts to move, keep your knees together and your skis parallel.

6 Your arms should be straight, but slightly bent at the elbows.

7 Press forward lightly with both feet.

8 Stay in a sitting position until the boat pulls you out of the water.

9 When your skis are horizontal to the water, stand. Even when standing upright, be sure to keep your knees slightly bent to act as shock absorbers.

DOS AND DON'TS

1 Do adjust your skis so they feel snug on your feet.

2 Don't adjust your skis so tightly that they won't come off in a fall.

3 Don't stand too soon, or you will be thrown off balance and fall.

4 Don't pull the rope toward your body.

5 Do keep your arms straight.

6 Don't look upward to avoid getting sprayed in the face. Looking at the boat will help you keep a balanced position.

7 Don't look down at your skis.

8 Do keep your back straight with your skis shoulder-width apart.

9 Do stay inside the wakes until you get a feel for waterskiing.

DON'T **FLIP** OUT

Take it slow. Get a feel for how waterskiing works. Then you can start learning the tricks of the trade. Start by crossing the wakes and work your way toward the fancy stuff. Once you've mastered the art of waterskiing, you might give slalom a try (swinging out on both sides of the boat in wide sweeps, ideally creating a "rooster tail" of water when turning). Wakeboarding (see the previous section) and kneeboarding (similar to wakebordring, but you kneel on the board) are fun, too. If you're really ambitious, barefoot skiing is next.

TIPS:

- Let the skis and the boat do the work. Staying within the boat's wake will give you a smoother ride if there are other boats around.

- Let go of the rope when you fall. This will only take one time to learn.

- Use hand signals to communicate with the driver: Thumbs up for more speed, thumbs down for less speed, and give a wave to let the driver know you're okay after a fall.

For the best tips, techniques, and latest buzz on all things water skiing, check out www.waterskimag.com, **the official site of** *Water Ski Magazine.* **Subscribe by calling 800-879-0495 or send an email to** waterski@palmcoastd.com.

Tom King/Water Ski Magazine

BAREFOOTING: HOW TO GET STARTED

Once the skis are out of the way, you'll still need a few things. A barefoot suit with plenty of padding and built in flotation is a must. Barefoot padded shorts to wear beneath your barefoot suit are not critical, but when you're learning you'll be grateful for the extra padding. Slalom gloves aren't mandatory either but, again, they make for a more comfortable experience. Don't forget the most important items—a basic barefoot handle and a low-stretch main line.

You won't need a license if you're just barefooting for fun, although making sure your instructor has one isn't a bad idea. The American Barefoot Club (ABC) is a division of USA Water Ski. Any licenses that are granted come from USA Water Ski.

Lessons can be bought at package rates and will cost something like 10 for $200. Included in that cost, along with the lessons, is all the necessary gear you'll need to learn. After you get the hang of the sport, you may want to join a club. You'll pay fees the same as you would at a gym, and you can go barefootin' to your toes' content.

LEARNING TO BAREFOOT

Basically, you have to be going pretty fast to skim across the water on your bare feet. To figure out exactly how fast you should be going, divide your weight by ten, then add twenty. If you weigh 160 pounds, you would need to be going 36 mph, which is fast on water.

There are many ways to learn to barefoot, but most experts recommend starting on a boom, or a rigid pole that juts out to the side of the boat. You can hold it like a handle and learn by skiing beside the boat.

Learning on a Boom:

- You'll start by hanging onto the boom as you would from a bar if you were doing a pull-up. The driver will start the boat moving forward.
- The motion of the boat will make your legs begin to drag behind you, the water hitting you at your thighs.
- As the driver pushes the boat gradually to a higher speed, be sure to hang on to that boom!
- You'll feel the water's surface getting harder as the boat picks up speed. That is your signal to begin to turn your body to one side, so the water is hitting your hip.
- Pull your knees up so they are at about 90 degrees, and swing the lower half of your body around in front of you. At this point, you'll basically be squatting on the water's surface.
- Now place your heels on the water and almost instantly you will stand up!

For beginners, calm water makes learning much, much easier, but what's most vital to planing is posture. After all, if your body isn't positioned correctly, you'll lose your balance and fall immediately.

The Ideal Barefoot Stance:
- Feet shoulder-width apart
- Knees bent at almost 90 degrees
- Arms straight
- Head up
- Hips forward

Once you've mastered the basics of the sport, you can start to learn tricks. Get a feel for the fancy stuff by learning to cross the wakes. First take a deep breath. Then, start just outside the curl. Gently and steadily apply your weight to the outside foot, and be sure to keep your toes up as you use your momentum to carry you across the wake. Get comfortable with those wakes and you'll be doing one-foots before you know it!

If you graduate to competition, there are all kinds of challenges. For example, barefoot jumping has strict requirements. The takeoff edge of the ramp is about 18 inches above the water line. Jumpers must be barefoot by the time they reach a step-off buoy, located 165 feet before the ramp. They must maintain a barefooting position into the ramp and are judged on distance. Look, Ma, I'm flying.

Tom King/*Water Ski Magazine*

Tom King/*Water Ski Magazine*

PADDLE ON: WHITEWATER CANOEING AND KAYAKING

to keep in mind that boaters should never attempt to run rivers solo. Adhering to the buddy system could save your life in the event of an emergency. But when the water churns and the waves splash, you'll be alone enough in your boat—testing your skills and mettle against the muscle power of a force of nature.

There's nothing quite like the rush of racing wildly through whitewater rapids in a canoe or kayak, dodging rocks, and dropping over killer water falls, emerging dripping wet, then spinning your boat and finding safety in a downstream eddy, the adrenaline pumping through your veins—that is, if you make it.

Whitewater paddling in canoes or kayaks is essentially an individual sport, but it's good

GEARING UP

Beginners should consider contacting a local enthusiasts' club to get started. Outfitting yourself with the proper equipment can be confusing and expensive. There are so many styles of boats to choose from, and not all are suitable for beginners. And, as with any sport, there's a broad range of prices and options when it comes to equipment. Paddles, boats, and other gear are made from a variety of materials to suit a variety of needs. The advice of a seasoned veteran—especially one with no financial stake in your selections—can be invaluable.

With that in mind, you also can begin your quest for whitewater heaven at a local outfitter or sporting goods store. Many such stores carry at least some paddling supplies, and some offer limited instruction or equipment rentals. While there, you'll also be able to assess the substantial dough that will be required of you should you decide to pursue the sport beyond a weekend/rented-equipment basis. Perhaps more important, you may be able to gather information about local paddling clubs or individuals who may be willing to get you started. Many neophyte paddlers get their first taste of whitewater excitement running a formidable river in a raft with a commercial outfitter.

The popularity of the sport has increased steadily over the years, and many rafters graduate to the thrills of navigating rapids and surfing holes in their own canoes or kayaks.

WHAT TO EXPECT

If you've never experienced the thrill of running rapids, you're in for a special treat. (The log-flume ride at your local amusement park doesn't count, either.) Once you "put on" a river, there's an element of freedom—and danger—that no theme park could (or would ever want to) reproduce, no matter how tame the river may be.

Speaking of tameness: Rapids in North America are classified according to a scale ranging from Class I to Class VI.

Getting Started: Equipment

Before drenching yourself, you'll need the following essential items:

• A whitewater kayak or whitewater canoe (decked or open-hulled) with appropriate internal flotation. Please note: Flat-water canoes and touring or sea kayaks are not generally suitable for running rapids. Decked whitewater canoes are called "C-boats." While they resemble kayaks, they are essentially canoes with cockpits. C-boat paddlers sit on their knees and use a one-bladed paddle, as open-hull canoeists do. Kayakers' legs are extended, and they use a double-bladed paddle.

• A Personal Flotation Device (PFD), or life vest. Look for a well-fitting PFD that is specially designed for the sport.

• A double-bladed paddle, suitable for your height (for kayakers), or a single-bladed paddle (for canoeists).

• A spray skirt, which seals the cockpit, for kayakers and C-boaters.

• A helmet.

Additional equipment that may enhance your experience:

• Polypropylene, nylon, and/or neoprene clothing, including wetsuits, drysuits, "rubber" booties, windproof paddling jackets, etc. (Note: You should never wear cotton in water. It absorbs water, weighs you down, and does not retain warmth. If you absolutely cannot afford the more expensive clothing, wear wool or synthetic fibers whenever possible.)

• Waterproof storage bags/containers for snacks, drinks, sunscreen, valuables, etc.

• A waterproof camera and/or spare film.

• A throw rope (a self-contained heavy-duty rope for river rescues).

• A whistle. May be useful for calling for help in an emergency.

• A diving knife. Useful for cutting yourself free in the unlikely—but potentially life-threatening—event of a pinning accident.

• Sunglasses with reliable retainer straps.

• Sunscreen.

• Spare paddles (for open canoes).

• Plenty of fresh drinking water.

• Cash and/or coins for unexpected emergencies off river.

• A first-aid kit for unexpected emergencies on river.

• A small flashlight and lighter or matches for emergencies.

• River running guidebooks and maps for the area you will be paddling.

Class I water consists of a few tame riffles with no obstructions. You could float down these in an inner tube.

Class II rapids present more challenges. Waves are up to three feet high, but channels are wide and obvious.

Class III rapids require some skill to navigate. They feature high, irregular waves, and narrow passages that require maneuvering, and some may require on-shore scouting.

Class IV rapids should only be tackled by experienced boaters. These rapids include long, turbulent, narrow passages, which may require scouting from shore, particularly if you are unfamiliar with the river. Paddlers attempting to run these rapids should have a reliable Eskimo roll, a maneuver that allows a boater who has overturned his craft to return to an upright position without exiting the cockpit. (There's instruction on how to do it at the end of this section.)

Class V rapids are considered to be at the edge of safe navigability, even for experienced boaters. Rapids in this class are extremely violent and routes are extremely steep. They should always be scouted from shore. Rescue is considered problematic, and there is a significant danger in the event of a mishap.

Class VI rapids are considered "nearly impossible and extremely dangerous," according to the American Whitewater Affiliation. Most boaters elect to carry their boats (portage) around these stretches whenever possible.

Most recreational rivers feature a blend of Class II and Class III rapids, often with calm pools between drops. The good news is that running rapids takes far more skill and finesse than brute strength; some of the best whitewater paddlers are women. To be sure, some conditioning and raw muscle power are essential to successful navigation in tricky waters. But precise technique, honed by countless hours of practice, is the true key to success. The best paddlers learn how to work with the awesome power of the water, rather than fight it. Experienced paddlers learn how to "read" the rapids, discerning potential trouble spots and mentally plotting downstream routes. They learn to recognize seemingly hidden dangers, how to anticipate the characteristics of hydraulics, and how to hop between the safe havens of eddies (the places where calm water flows back upstream, usually behind rocks or logs or a bend in the river).

KNOW YOUR CRAFT

There are crucial differences between whitewater craft and most everything else. Unlike sea kayaks or touring kayaks, whitewater kayaks and canoes are designed for agility rather than stability. They are able to turn in an instant—an important advantage when negotiating tricky, rock-strewn rapids—but the trade-off for agility means they are relatively easy to tip over.

Maneuvering a whitewater craft also relies on keeping the craft relatively watertight. Although kayaks and C-boats use inflatable floatation bags fore and aft of the boater, waterlogged boats become ponderous, difficult-to-steer bathtubs. Kayaks and C-boats use tightly fitting spray skirts. Worn snugly around a boater's waist, the spray skirt is stretched to fit the rim of the cockpit, sealing the boater in and keeping water out. If the boat capsizes and the boater must "ditch," "swim," or "wet exit" (all terms that really mean "swimming for your life"), the skirt is easily and quickly disengaged from the cockpit by pulling on a grab loop designed for that purpose.

ROLL LIKE AN ESKIMO

Because capsizing is inevitable, the Inuits of the Arctic Circle perfected an up-righting maneuver hundreds of years ago in their sealskin and whalebone kayaks. Known to us as the "Eskimo roll," the maneuver enables a kayaker, and even a skilled canoeist, to flip his craft back upright without the danger and trouble of making a wet exit. While the maneuver is remarkably simple to execute once learned, it's the learning part that's tricky. But with guidance from an experienced paddler, and perseverance, you can learn an essential skill that should be mastered before attempting any rapids beyond Class III. Many whitewater clubs hold indoor pool roll training sessions in the winter, an excellent time to prepare for the high waters that come with spring rains.

READY, SET, ROLL

To start, find some fairly shallow water or a swimming pool, about three to five feet deep, and enlist a friend to help. Your friend is there basically to pull you out if you panic underwater.

The first step to learn is how to make a successful wet exit. To do this, hold your breath, flip your boat over, then lean far forward. Grab the loop in front of you, located on the spray skirt, in the middle of the cockpit rim. Yank it, unsealing your spray skirt. Tumble forward and exit your boat. It is crucial that you lean and roll *forward*. Unfortunately, leaning forward while trapped underwater, in what suddenly feels like a floating coffin, goes against your instincts, especially for neophytes. Resist the urge to lean back. The key to a clean escape (and no scraped skin) is rolling forward.

The next step is learning the "high brace." This simple maneuver when executed properly allows you to avoid capsizing in the first place! Holding your paddle at about chest level, reach out to the right, twisting your wrist so the flat face of the blade can slap the water. (If you fail to turn the paddle, it will slice into the water and you'll get dunked.) Now raise your left arm, elbow still bent, and place the blade in the

Measuring the Strength of a River

It's important to understand that a river can change dramatically depending upon the height the water has reached and how fast it is flowing. What's easily navigable at one height may become perilous at another.

The "strength" of a river's current is calculated in two ways: Measuring the river's height in feet (usually marked by a gauge painted on a bridge pylon or riverside rock), or by recording its actual flow rate, as measured in cubic feet per second or CFS. (A flooding river can run at rates of 30,000 cubic feet per second.)

Most recreational rivers have well-known flow rates and/or levels, and are usually obtainable by calling local sources. West Virginia's New River, for instance, is virtually ideal at a height of about three to four feet. Huge waves come in uninterrupted "trains," and surfing holes abound.

The river remains navigable even at minus one foot, but at that level drops are more likely to scrape the bottom of your boat, and the overall experience is less of a thrill than running at higher levels. If it's too high, rapids may wash out, and putting in is only recommended for highly experienced paddlers. As small streams flood, the risk of being snagged by tree limbs or submerged obstacles, such as fences, increases. These "strainers" pose a serious threat, and eddies (areas of slowly moving, upstream-flowing water that develop behind obstructions) may be few and far between.

can also be practiced in a shallow river or pond with help from a friend standing in the water who provides a "ledge" to lean on.

Once you've gained confidence in your hip snap, you're ready to attempt a roll. The key word here is "attempt."

Assuming you are right handed, lean far forward. Rotate your arms and wrists to place the paddle beside (parallel with) the boat on your right. Rotate your wrists as far forward as possible, and strive to shove the paddle as far down as possible. That's because, in a moment, down will be up, and you'll want the paddle to be on *top* of the water, in the ready position.

Now comes the moment of truth: With your friend at the ready, flip your boat over. Leaning far forward, keeping the wrists bent forward, attempt as best you can to relax, and let the end of the paddle break free of the water above. Now, with a sweeping motion, bring your arms in an arc back around to a ready position (facing forward, arms in front of you, hands at about shoulder width apart, paddle held level, perpendicular to the boat; all this is happening while you are underwater and upside down). As you feel your paddle sweeping the surface of the water above, snap your hips and plunge the face of your paddle blade into the water, flipping yourself up with a high brace. With any luck (and maybe a little help from the person gripping the end of the boat) you should now be upright, without ever leaving your boat. Chances are it won't be quite that easy, but practice will pay off when your head is scraping the bottom of some river and you pop up like a cork, heading downstream like a pro.

water beside you, perhaps a foot or two from the cockpit. Lean to the right, then push yourself back upright by leaning on the paddle and pulling it toward the cockpit. Practice this maneuver on both sides, gradually increasing the degree of tip-over. You'll probably be surprised at how far you can tip to one side, while pushing against the water with the flat of your blade, without capsizing.

You can simulate the effects of waves in the following exercise. Ask a friend to stand in shallow water and grab your stern (back end of your boat), then have him attempt to flip you over. By bracing yourself as your friend tries to drench you, you'll learn to react quickly and to stay upright.

Now that you know you can exit your capsized boat without drowning, and you've mastered the high brace, you're ready to learn the hip snap.

In a swimming pool, pull your boat alongside the wall. Grab the wall, then stretch your arms out, tipping your boat all the way over. The seam (side) of your boat should be pointing straight up; your torso should be half submerged. Now, with a snap of the hips, bring the boat back upright. Try to do this without relying on your arms. The point is to get back up with hip action alone. Practice this move on both sides. The hip snap

THE RUSH OF RAFTING

SURPLUS START

In the past three decades or so, whitewater rafting has grown from a handful of mom-and-pop operations to literally hundreds of companies vying for eager customers. Interest in the sport was sparked after the end of World War II, when Army surplus life rafts were used by returning vets to have fun on wild rivers. Some began taking adventurous friends along, and eventually, paying clients.

As technology improved and interest in this exhilarating sport grew, fledgling outfitters became more sophisticated, offering more variety and improved safety measures. In the past few decades the sport has experienced an unprecedented increase in popularity due, in part, to outfitters' savvy marketing and rave word-of-mouth reviews from satisfied (and often repeat) customers.

Drawn irresistibly to the adventure of pulse-pounding rivers, adrenaline junkies were outfitters' first and most enthusiastic customers. They're still around, but today outfitters' clients are more likely to be mainstream middle Americans than in the past. Clients range in age from five to 85 these days, and there are even special trips tailored to meet the needs of handicapped people.

TAKE A NUMBER, PLEASE

All of this popularity has created a crowd on some of the best rivers. At the height of the rafting season in October, West Virginia's Gauley River—

arguably the best whitewater river east of the Mississippi—more closely resembles a crowded interstate highway leading out of Manhattan at rush hour than a scenic waterway coursing through the wilderness. Countless rafts compete for space in football field-sized eddies. They're all jockeying for position and a chance to approach the first drops of some of the stupendous rapids, which have made the Gauley so popular. So much for getting away from it all.

Likewise, if you wish to navigate the mighty Colorado River through the Grand Canyon, be sure to plan well ahead. Waiting lists have been known to stretch out for years, and no one is allowed on the river without a permit issued by the National Park Service. The good news is that despite such runaway success, outfitters have not lost sight of the original goal: to get your arms working and your heart racing, to soak you thoroughly, and to take you on a thrill ride you hardly imagined possible—and, of course, to survive to tell the story. If you have to sample some gourmet cuisine along the way, sleep under the stars, and sip fine wine around a campfire at night, try to make the best of it.

FOR STARTERS

If you live somewhere essentially flat, such as Florida or Oklahoma, for instance, you'll need to travel to the nearest mountain range for exciting rafting that amounts to more than a slow float downstream. In North America that means, essentially, the Appalachian Mountain range in the East, and the Rockies and Sierras in the West.

One of the oldest and best-known outfitters in the country, if not the world, is the Nantahala Outdoor Center (NOC), located adjacent to the Nantahala River in western North Carolina. The NOC

possible, therefore, to schedule trips on the "Nanty" not only during the rainy spring and fall seasons, but also throughout the summer, when other rivers are trickling, un-runnable rock gardens.

Other outfitters are scattered throughout the hills and mountains of North America, on formidable rivers such as the New and Gauley, in West Virginia, the Lehigh in the Poconos of Pennsylvania, the Chatooga in Georgia, and the Big South Fork in Tennessee. In the West, you'll find powerful rivers such as the Salmon and Snake in Idaho; the American, Merced, and Stanislaus in California; the Yampa and the Green in Utah; or the mighty Colorado, cutting a swath through the Grand Canyon in Arizona.

WHAT YOU'LL NEED

The good news about whitewater rafting is that outfitters exist to attend to your every need. Depending upon the level of challenge posed by a given river, outfitters may place certain restrictions on customers. For instance, highly technical, difficult—and yes, dangerous—rivers, such as West Virginia's awesome Upper Gauley, demand that rafters have a certain level of proficiency. Most reputable outfitters require proof that clients have at least some previous

also runs expeditions on five other notable rivers in the Southern Appalachian Mountains. The Nantahala River itself is a popular river especially suited to first-time rafters. Controlled by dam-release flows, its relatively tame rapids are not dependent upon rainfall or snow melting, in contrast to many other popular rivers. It's

whitewater experience before allowing them to tackle the 15-foot drops and meteor-size holes encountered on this notoriously exciting, but formidable, river. Age restrictions may also apply on certain other difficult or risky rivers, but many are tame enough that no such restrictions are imposed.

One item you will definitely need is cash. Rafting trips vary widely in terms of cost, depending on a variety of factors, ranging from the outfitter you choose to the type or length of trip you desire. But none come cheaply.

During spring and fall, and on cold, dam-release rivers such as the Ocoee in Tennessee, or the Nantahala in North Carolina, it's important to dress warmly. Wool is best if you do not own neoprene or polypropylene. (Many outfitters rent or sell neoprene wet suits, and polypropylene and nylon paddling clothes.) Other synthetic fibers may also be suitable, but avoid cotton. Except in high summer, jeans and T-shirts are not recommended; they are heavy and cold when wet. Athletic shoes are acceptable footwear, provided you don't mind them getting soggy. But specialized river shoes are ideal. Forget going barefoot.

As competition has stiffened among outfitting companies, their focus on customer satisfaction has prompted an almost fanatical attention to customer-friendly details. Most pride themselves on providing excellent on- and off-river meals, ranging from simply good to gourmet.

You may choose between half-day, all-day, and multi-day trips. Comfortable campgrounds and on-site stores are the norm, and many rivers even support hotels for the convenience of more comfort-conscious clients.

BE PREPARED

Rafts come in a variety of sizes, ranging from small four-man crafts to huge boats designed to carry 18 people and withstand powerful, punishing rivers that require days to descend. These rugged boats also hold enormous loads of gear. Most commercial craft fit somewhere in between, seating about a dozen boaters. Clients are expected to sit on the gunwales (top of the sides), hooking their feet as best they can under the inflated tubes that make up the hull.

Never ever attempt to tie yourself into the boat. Inexperienced boaters often crave the security of being restrained in some manner, but this is a recipe for disaster should the boat capsize. Paddlers who get tangled in

ropes can drown, and many have. If a raft capsizes, you must be free to swim clear of the craft immediately. Most paddlers eventually learn to stride the gunwales as if they're riding a horse, absorbing the bucking up-and-down motion of the craft with their feet firmly planted and knees deeply bent.

It's always possible, however, for a rafter to lose his grip and be thrown clear of the boat. (Some even consider this to be the fun part.) In any event, don't

panic. Your floatation device will keep you afloat. In the meantime as you flail in the water and yell "HELP!!!" try to hold onto your paddle, and pull your knees to your chest and keep your feet in front of you. Face downstream if at all possible, especially if you are in rapids. This is important: Never allow your feet to drift beneath you. They may catch on a submerged rock, and the current could pull you under. With your knees tucked in to your chest and your feet in front of you,

Whitewater Rafting USA

Eastern United States outfitters:

North American River Runners (West Virginia*)
1 (800) 950-2585
www.narr.com

Class VI River Runners (West Virginia*)
1 (800) 252-7784
www.800classvi.com

Nantahala Outdoor Center (North Carolina*)
1 (800) 232-7232
www.noc.com

Southeastern Expeditions (Georgia*)
1 (800) 868-7238
www.southeasternexpeditions.com

Rafting in the Smokies (Tennessee*)
1 (800) 776-7238
www.raftinginthesmokies.com

Zoar Outdoor (Massachusetts*)
1 (800) 532-7483
www.zoaroutdoor.com

Western United States outfitters:

Western River Expeditions (Utah*)
1 (800) 453-7475
www.westernriver.com

OARS—Outdoor Adventure River Specialists (California*)
1 (800) 346-6277
www.oars.com/home

ROW—River Odysseys West (Idaho*)
1 (800) 451-6034
www.rowinc.com

Outdoor Adventures (California*)
1 (800) 323-4234
www.gorafting.com

Echo—the Wilderness Company (California*)
1 (800) 652-3246
www.echotrips.com

*Denotes a company's home base. Many companies operate trips and/or outposts in other states, and internationally. A comprehensive whitewater river rafting referral guide is located online at: www.riversearch.com

while using his or her own paddle as a rudder to steer. You will be expected to paddle forward and backward, although the momentum of the river's current should do most of the work.

Paddling is not a particularly difficult skill, but you and your fellow rafters have to work at it. If you are seated on the right side of the craft, grip your paddle's handle firmly in your left hand, and loosely grip the shaft with your right. Reaching over the gunwales of the raft, reach as far ahead of you as is comfortable and dip your paddle into the water. The concave face of the paddle should be toward you, and the face should be inserted into the water perpendicular to the direction of travel. Pull straight back, alongside the craft. As you bring your paddle beside you, or slightly behind you, twist the shaft 90 degrees and remove it from the water in a clean, smooth motion. Reaching forward again, and rotating the shaft back to the perpendicular, dig forward for your next stroke.

Avoid sinking your paddle either too much or too little. Ideally, the water should be about an inch or two below the point where the flat blade tapers into the shaft. Use a strong, steady pulling motion to be most effective.

you will be able to push off of any obstacles you hit. In most cases, you'll be able to quickly regain entry into the boat with the help of fellow paddlers. So be nice to your comrades, so they don't debate over whether to pull you in.

BE THE PADDLE

It helps to be in good enough physical condition that you're able to rise to the challenge of paddling hard when necessary. Provided you have not opted for an oar-boat, which is powered solely by guides, you will be expected to pitch in and paddle for all you're worth. That's because in whitewater, the boat is controlled by moving faster or slower than the current.

You will receive instructions on the finer points of working as a team and stroking on command. Perched in the stern of the raft, your guide will issue orders,

5
SNOWED

If you visit or live in a northern climate, and you have the privilege of the wind blowing icicles onto your eyebrows, you can either complain about it until your friends seal your mouth shut with frozen water, or you can make an Xtreme sport out of it. We suggest the latter.

Fast snow sports run the range from the once sneered-at snowboarding, which has now been elevated to a spot in the Olympics, to skeleton and bobsledding, which reach speeds of more than 90 mph, not to mention Xtreme skiing, in which the speed record stands at more than 140 mph. And some of the places these skiers frequent are so out-of-the-way, only a polar bear could love them. It's all speed and slope—and the numbness, of course. Learn to love it.

SKIING
ON THE EDGE

Hardcore skiers think of Xtreme skiing as a sport that pushes them dangerously closer to the abyss than they've ever been before.

It can involve descents down previously unconquered mountain faces, where the extraordinarily steep and dangerous runs are accessible only by helicopter or mountain climbing; some runs demand a combination of skiing and rappelling—skills honed by a cross-trained athlete with a lot of stamina and even more guts.

And by some definitions, Xtreme skiing also encompasses adrenaline-rich offshoots, such as ultra-high altitude skiing—Xtreme skiers have made descents of peaks (including Mount Everest) that exceed a lung-bursting 20,000 feet.

Speed skiing falls in this Xtreme category too. In 1999, Austrian Harry Egger won the world speed skiing title in Les Arcs, France, when he screamed down the course at an amazing 154 mph. Egger is hailed as the fastest athlete on earth (motorized records excepted). In truth, the athlete at that speed never even touches the snow; he's planing on air.

"Extreme skiing is about skiing that is so difficult, if you make one mistake, you're over," says 1995

World Extreme Skiing Champion Dean Cummings. "It involves picking routes that are so steep and dangerous that if you take a roll you just unhook from the mountain; you just touch [the mountain face] every 100 feet or so."

Or put another way: "If you fall, you die," he says.

There are really only a handful of elite Xtreme skiers in the world. Pioneered by Europeans with a strong tradition of mountaineering skills, Xtreme skiing today is really about skiing what's perceived as un-skiable. Some enthusiasts claim to have summoned the courage to attack steep slopes, called *couloirs*, of 65 degrees or more. (Derived from the French word for "slide," a couloir is a deep mountainside gorge or gully with steep, narrow sides.) Although these occur within the boundaries of some major ski resorts (Corbet's Couloir at Jackson Hole in Wyoming, for one), they often are very remote. (Cummings challenges reports of skiers who have tackled 65 degree faces, as some have claimed. "Sixty degrees is the limit of what's doable," Cummings says. "If sustained, [65°] is not realistic.")

Whatever your definition, there's little doubt that this is a sport for experts. Intermediate skiers who've never left the confines of a lift-serviced, ski-patrolled ski resort clearly have no business in out-of-bounds backcountry areas making breakneck descents through dangerous chutes at oxygen-starved altitudes. This is a sport for the serious, well-trained skier, an athlete who is at the peak of his mental and physical abilities, one who craves the challenge of successfully skiing previously untamed terrain in a near straight vertical descent.

RISKY BUSINESS

Discouraged yet? Here are some more warnings. Despite the popularity of movies and television commercials that glorify Xtreme skiing, avalanche prevention specialists and ski safety experts warn the inexperienced to reconsider before considering a run in the big out-of-bounds. Death is not uncommon.

Although contact with boulders at speeds approaching 100 mph is clearly a danger, that's not an Xtreme skier's worst fear. The risk of avalanche in areas where Xtreme skiing is commonly pursued is also an ever-present hazard. Obviously, helmets are highly recommended, as is training in avalanche survival. Xtreme skiers should never head into unpatrolled areas without avalanche survival training and equipment. And out-of-bounds skiing should never ever be attempted alone. At these high altitudes, hypothermia, frostbite, severe sunburn, and dehydration are common.

WANT TO TRY IT? HERE'S WHERE

Still want to try it? Here's a way to get a taste without dying. Heli-skiing (skiing in areas only accessible by helicopter) and other forms of backcountry, or off-piste skiing (skiing in uncharted areas) are not restricted to competition-level experts. Many heli-skiing clients have little or no avalanche training and advanced-intermediate to advanced skiing skills. While commercial heli-skiing is not the outer limit of Xtreme skiing, it is near the edge and can put you on virgin snow in some of the most beautiful country in the world.

For example, H2O Heli Adventures has access to 1,500 square miles of pristine wilderness in Alaska. Snowfall reaches as much as 60 to 80 *feet* of snow per year and a mere 3 percent of peaks have even been named in this vast skiers' playground.

Clients ski off huge, vertical mountains. Despite relatively low peak altitudes in the Chugach Mountains—the highest is approximately a still-respectable 13,000-feet—vertical drops run between 2,000 and 5,000 feet because the Chugach Range descends directly down to sea level. Base of operations is Valdez, which sits on Prince William Sound.

Clients can expect to tackle up to 20,000 feet of vertical skiing each day, making about six runs per day at about 3,000 to 4,000 feet per run. They ski with certified guides and carry avalanche survival gear, including backpacks and probes, digital transceivers, shovels, and radios.

safer elevations accessible by snowcat
(a cross between a snow mobile and
a bulldozer), or to pursue other
sports, such as sea or whitewater
kayaking until conditions improve.

For more information, these are
some contacts:

• H2O Heli Adventures:
www.h2oguides.com; (800) 578-HELI.

• Akuni Adventures: www.akuni.com;
(416) 410-7240.

• Alaska Backcountry Adventures:
www.alaskabackcountry.com; (907) 835-5608.

• City and Outport Adventures:
www.newfoundlandtours.com/cityandoutport;
(709) 754-8687.

• Great Canadian Adventure Company:
www.adventures.ca; (888) 285-1676.

• Jackson Hole Heli-Ski Adventure:
www.tetonpines.com/heli.shtml; (800) 238-2223.

• R.K. Heli-Skiing Adventures: www.rkheliski.com;
(800) 661-6060.

• Wilderness Adventure Company:
www.wildernessadventure.com; (888) 849-7668.

Skiers hoping to
tackle the backcountry of Alaska should be proficient at
kick turns, sidestepping, and making steep traverses.
They must also learn rope skills, and will undergo a
brief avalanche survival orientation. Snow conditions are
always carefully monitored. If avalanche conditions exist
at higher elevations, clients are encouraged to ski lower,

SNOWBOARDING: THIS ALL STARTED WITH TWO SKIS NAILED TOGETHER?

"What the hell is that?" That's what many skiing snobs asked when some bright bulb decided to nail two skis together, hit the slopes at breakneck speeds, and introduce a sport that now boasts more than a million riders in the U.S., a World Cup Tour, and a spot in the Winter Olympics.

The snowboarding craze that exploded on America's ski slopes in the 1980s has made it easier and quicker, not to mention a heck of a lot more fun, for people to enjoy the slippery peaks of snow-covered mountains. But the ride down has not always been pure powder when it came to mixing traditional skiers and Xtreme boarders.

As snowboarding grew in popularity, many resorts resisted the trend. They thought the mutant mix of traditional skiing, surfing, and skateboarding was an abomination. The only thing more absurd was—gasp—sledding! Early snowboarders were the outcasts of the slopes. Eventually, after the profit-minded ski resort operators saw the error of their ways, the sport began to be accepted. Now even Aspen's finest cater to the snowboarding crowd.

GEARING UP
–HIT THE MOUNTAIN WITH THE RIGHT EQUIPMENT

The right gear for your trek can mean the difference between a fun time and an unbearable misadventure—not to mention the chance of frostbite. More important, though, is looking cool while you snowboard, a key to finding a ski bunny or mountain man at the lodge later. What follows are rules of thumb that are standard throughout the sport. Use them as guides, but talk to store employees and other boarders.

We'll begin this run with some general advice about equipment. Starting at the bottom, here is what to look for.

Boards

There's a huge range of boards. Some offer more flex than others, some are better suited for jumps, while still others are designed to carve like a Ginsu knife. Most are generally constructed with some combination of wood and plastic, but high-end sticks boast neat things like carbon- and titanium-reinforcing ingredients. For now, ignore all of that stuff and the sales people who say you need it. Unless your picture is in a magazine, don't waste the money.

As a beginner, the best choice is to find an all-around board that works well in any condition. After you get the basics down, you'll be launching airs in no time, so you don't want to be stranded with a stick that can't handle your improvement. Your height and weight are the biggest factors in choosing a board. When standing with the board resting against your chest, the tip should be between your chin and the top of your sternum (that's your breastbone).

The width of the board is important as well, but for practical reasons. If you have gunboats for feet, you are going to need a wider board. If those cannons at the bottom of your ankles hang over the sides, your toes and ankles may dig into the snow when you throw down deep turns. Keep in mind, though, a wider board will be tougher to transition from edge to edge (something we'll cover later).

Boots

Many of today's boots look like what NASA issues to its space boys. They may be bulky and awkward to walk in, but they'll keep your toes toasty, and that's what matters. The biggest improvement in boots are better linings, which mean more comfort and warmth. Find a pair that feels good and that fits snugly. A loose fitting boot will not only cost you some heat on your feet, you'll also lose some control in your turns.

Bindings

As the name implies, this piece of equipment attaches, or binds, you to your board. Finding the right pair is a combination of what type of riding you'll be doing, comfort, and convenience. So here goes:

Step-ins

These models require specially designed boots to work. The clips on your board attach to small metal pieces on the bottom of your shoe and hold you firmly to the board. These are a great choice for new riders who will be in and out of the bindings all day. They make getting around between lifts much easier.

Strap-ins

These offer a bit more support and are the choice of more experienced riders. Boarders who attack the parks or who are making big jumps prefer the strap-ins and the way they firmly attach to the board. They won't help with the hospital bills after a heavy crash, but at least you'll still have your board.

SLIDING HIGH

If you have ever surfed or ridden a skateboard, deciding which way you ride will be easy. If you ride with your left foot forward, you are said to ride regular-footed. If you prefer your right foot in front, you ride goofy-footed. Neither is better, and don't get hung up on the goofy thing. It's just a way to tell the difference.

The biggest complaint beginners have is the awkward feeling of both feet being strapped on a single board, rather than on two separate skis. You know what? Get used to it. And you do, quite quickly. After two dozen falls in the first run, the board will be a part of you.

Another hump you'll soon find is that getting around between lifts and runs can require a talent all its own. The key is releasing just your back foot while leaving your front foot attached. You may look like Quasimodo after too many cocktails, but you don't earn style points here. This is all about function. Push off with your rear foot and glide whenever possible. There will be some hopping, a couple of spills, and lots of apologies to other riders, but you'll quickly get the hang of it.

CHASING RABBITS

Don't let either your friends' peer pressure or your own ego convince you that only wimps ride the bunny trail. Ninty-nine percent of riders blazing down the slopes started on the kiddie hill. You should too. For one, it's safer. You're less likely to get crushed by the maniacs who test gravity's full potential with every run. Two, you'll add some years to your life by avoiding the frustration that comes from trying to ride a hill you're not ready for.

After you successfully depart from the lift (count getting off the lift a victory), you will fall and embarrass yourself the first 10 times. Everyone does. Don't sweat it. The first step is to learn to slide down on your heel, or back, edge. This is the easiest way to control both your speed and direction. With your shoulders square to the slope, work on balancing on your heels and using your weight to change direction. Sounds easy, right? Grown men have been seen weeping, and women heard cursing like dock workers at this stage. Don't worry though, you'll pick it up quickly.

Keep these two simple points in mind as your balance begins to improve: 1) Look where you want to go. 2) The feet follow where the shoulders lead. As you skid helplessly in one direction, turn your head and pick a spot where you want to slide. At the same time, adjust your shoulders and upper body toward the same spot. Pointing even helps. You'll realize that your feet, and the board, are just mindless

FALLING IS SUCH **SWEET** SORROW

There will be moments, after your bum has become way too friendly with the snow, that you'd rather just give up. Fight it. Although falling can be painful, when done correctly (yes, there is a right way to fall—never in front of a hot guy or girl!), it's possible to avoid serious injury.

When you biff, your mind will tell you to do certain things. For instance, when you tumble backward, the instinct is to toss your arms behind you to break your fall. DO NOT DO THIS! The only thing you're likely to break is your wrist, the most common injury among snowboarders.

Instead, when you're heading back (and you'll do this a lot), try to roll into a ball, tucking your arms in toward your body. An arm or a wrist can snap like dry timber, but it's surprising the abuse a body can take. If your face is heading for an unscheduled meeting with the snow, assume the "prayer position." Bend your knees, clasp your hands to your chest, and if the feeling strikes you, cry out, "Please God don't let me die!" The first two moves will definitely save you a trip to the emergency room. There's no clear report on the success rate of the third.

PUT THE **EDGE** ON

Eventually you'll abandon the safety of the heel edge of your board and start incorporating the front edge. It's like leaving home for the first time. You're excited, you don't know what to expect, it could be great, but you could also screw up big time.

Linking the two edges together is the foundation for mastering snowboarding. Watch any video and see how the pros transition between the two sides, effortlessly gliding down the face of pure powder, connecting turn after graceful turn. Your local mountain may not be as beautiful, or as empty, but your turns will be similar (at first, sort of like the way a Chihuahua and

drones, obeying what the upper body tells them.

You'll know it's time to bail from the bunny trail when you have mastered the "Falling Leaf." Although not as cool as a martial arts move, it's a basic maneuver that beginners need to know. Just picture a leaf after it has fallen from a tree, the way it glides back and forth though the air. You want to mimic the same motion, sliding side to side on your back edge.

a Saint Bernard are both dogs).

It's important for riders to keep their weight on one edge, as that's where the control lies. With the board pointed down the hill, begin sliding on your heelside, zigging across the face of the slope. Near the slope boundary, but not too close, work to switch your board to the opposite edge, zagging back over the face. It's not recommended that you get too close to those big green and brown things known as trees. They are hard, and they hurt when you hit them.

As you move on to the frontside, you'll feel like you're standing up on your toes. Making this transition between edges requires using both the upper body (remember the shoulders) and the back foot. From this point on, the back foot will play a big role in your riding.

ASSEMBLING THE PUZZLE PIECES

After a handful of runs, most of the skills you need will come as second nature, like a dancer and her routine. If ever you felt the need to show off your athletic prowess, this sport is the perfect choice for newcomers. The learning curve is short, and in half a day you can slide and carve enough to impress the folks at the lodge. And isn't that the real reason people snowboard?

GO BIG

Eventually, snowboarders want to move on and wave good-bye to the ground below. Jumps can be spectacular when they are executed with style and the landings nailed. They can also be a spectacle if you flop through the air and blow the landing.

When you attempt your first jump, think about your board never leaving the ground. In other words, act as if you are still cruising along on the snow.

This will keep the board on line when you touch back down. (This advice is for small jumps. It is not recommended that you attempt bigger ramps until you are an expert and wearing protective gear, namely a helmet.) Novice jumpers flub when they try to get too fancy, or start thinking, "Wow, I am off the ground." Just act as if you are still sliding. As you approach the jump, keep the board arrow straight, so you're not crooked in the air. When you do land, keep your knees bent and stay cool—"Yeah, that jump was no big deal"—as your heart bounces back from your stomach.

Another way to impress onlookers, and record a few bruises as well, is to take on the half-pipe at your local resort. Stealing shamelessly from the skateboard world, these giant snowy U-shaped ramps are ideal for launching huge air. The key to riding a pipe is the ability to ride switch-foot (that simply means being able to slide up and down the sides with either foot forward). This skill will come with time and, after a while, will seem second nature. A word of caution: Since half-pipes are not maintained the same way trails are, the snow is actually more like ice and can give you a nice beating. So take it slow your first few runs.

SKELETON SLEDDING & BOBSLEDDING: BONE-CHILLING SPEED

If you were lucky enough to grow up where there was lots of snow, you might have made your own toboggan run. You could pack down the snow, shovel up some banks, maybe even pour water down the hill, and ice over the run. The typical toboggan-loving child can travel about 10 to 15 mph down that hill. But what if you had the ultimate in frictionless sleds? What if you had the equivalent of a frozen waterslide, with perfectly smooth ice to slide down? What if you took a running start, head first, and reached speeds in excess of 75 miles mph. That's skeleton sledding, and it's not kids' stuff.

Then there's the team version—bobsledding. It attracts people from all walks of life, from royalty to the celebrated team from the snowless land of Jamaica. The speeds they reach are 90 mph plus, and that is smokin', mon.

SKELETONS PAST

Legend has it that the sport of skeleton sledding got its name from the look of the rickety sleds originally used back in the late 19th century. But you have to wonder if it just might also have had something to do with the bone-breaking speeds and death-defying danger that has become associated with the sport. Its start as an official competition apparently began in Switzerland, when the Winter Olympics were held there in 1928. Though its popularity was limited outside of Switzerland, an American, Jennison Heaton, was fastest in the first Olympic skeleton competition and took home the gold. In 1948 Italian newcomer Nino Bibbia again shocked the Swiss by winning the gold, and became the first skeleton superstar. He won 230 races in a row over 30 years, beaten finally by his son, Gianni, in 1975.

Today, 27 nations have official skeleton teams, and skeleton will be a primary Olympic sport at the Salt Lake Winter Olympics in 2002.

While bobsled and luge are considered the upper crust of Olympic snow sports, skeleton has long been the beer-swilling, tough-talking, black sheep of the sledding family. Skeleton sledders go down a bobsled run at more than 70 miles per hour, and they do it on their stomach, head first, three inches from the ice, with no steering and no brakes. So now you know why princes choose bobsledding instead.

WHAT IT'S LIKE

Many skeleton athletes get their start in bobsledding, and turn to the individual sport to find a new thrill. Danger is definitely the appeal; there's a serious adrenaline rush from being on the razor's edge.

The rules of skeleton allow a man's sled to be up to about 73 lbs., and a woman's can be about 64 lbs. There are no moving parts on the sled, and the sledder lies only from three to eight inches from the ground. The sleds are about four feet long and a little over a foot wide. So there's really not much there, thus the name.

Sleds are often refrigerated to be the same temperature as the ice, which minimizes friction. You run full-out with this 70-plus pound sled, at the top of a mountain bobsled run, then throw the sled onto the ice, and dive on top.

Okay, so you're on the ice, zipping down, gaining speed. You're using your body to lift and press down on the sled, shifting your balance and setting up your line through the upcoming curves. This is where you have milli-seconds to strategize. You have to think ahead, because the angle you take through the curves determines whether you achieve maximum speed or fly off the course like a missile. The entire run of more than 5,000 feet takes less than a minute.

OTHER GEAR

Skeleton competitors wear body suits that cut down on wind drag and have pads sewn in at all the right places. They often seem to be decorated in duct tape. It can be a slider's best friend, mending torn uniforms and protecting elbows and knees. Elbow pads are allowed, but not mandatory; helmets are, of course.

SPEEDING BULLET: THE BOBSLED

From Caribbean crews to crown princes, people attracted to bobsledding choose it for the unique sport that it is—the cherry on top of a winter sports ice cream sundae. But it is clearly not for everyone. Not only are you flying down an iced cement tube at 90 miles an hour, you're probably relying on somebody else to keep you alive. Remember Slim Pickens when he rode the atomic bomb from the belly of the airplane in *Dr. Strangelove?* Now you're getting the idea of what bobsledding is like, except you don't wear the rodeo hat, and you have teammates to go along.

THE JINGLING YOU'LL HEAR IS NOT FROM BELLS

For our purposes, let's call this sport bobsledding; the official, European and Olympic term is bobsleighing. Sleighs have little bells on them and are pulled by a couple of horses ready for the glue factory. Bing Crosby is associated with sleighs; bobsledding is more like rap.

There are three different roles for the speed junkies/athletes who participate in the sport of bobsledding.

Drivers, or pilots, are the captains of the team. They're the ones who get all of the glory and are sometimes well known for other things, such as their royal lineage. We'll get into that later. The drivers hop into the sled first and steer it on the way down. They're responsible for taking the best line and keeping the sled balanced. (They're also the only ones who don't have to hug another person.)

Brakemen (or brakewomen) load last. The term is pretty self-explanatory: They operate the brakes.

In four-man bobsled, the extra two men are known as pushers or push athletes. They are there for nothing but brute pushing force at the start. Athletes from other sports (pro football and track, just to name two) can find their way on to bobsled teams as pushers.

There are two sets of turns that exist on most of today's runs: the kreisel turn and the omega. A kreisel goes around a full 360 degrees, crossing underneath itself, like a cloverleaf. Omegas, which are shaped like the Greek omega symbol (Ω), whip the sled one way, then the other way, then back.

THE ORIGIN OF THE BOBSLED, EH?

Canadians say that loggers used bobsleds to haul their lumber for years. Montrealers had the "Tuque Bleue" slide in their city in the 1870s. The Brits also claim to have invented the bobsled, when a group of vacationing Englishmen raced their sleds in Davos, Switzerland, in 1890. About the same time in Albany, New York, bored lumberjacks raced their lumbersleds, jerry-rigged with rope steering and a garden rake for brakes.

Whatever. This much is known: The first steering mechanism attached to a bobsled was introduced in Switzerland. The first "bobsleigh" club was formed in St. Moritz in 1897, and five years later, the first bobsled-only run was built there.

In the early part of the 20th century, Europe experienced a bobsled craze. At one point, there were 60 bobsled runs in Switzerland. Kaiser Wilhelm of Germany, after a breeze in a bobsled, opened new runs in Germany. By 1914, more than 100 bobsled runs were endangering lives on the continent of Europe, a fitting prelude to World War I.

The four-man bob, although not the original version of the sport, was the first to be introduced as an Olympic sport, in 1924 in France. At the 1932 games in Lake Placid, the first two-man bob competition was held.

NOT YOUR GRANDFATHER'S BOBSLED

Today, bobsleds are $40,000 state-of-the-art fiberglass bullets, rocketing down iced tubes. There are 16 tracks around the world that host international competitions, and each is about a mile long with at least five turns. Nowadays, because of the speed and extreme turns, bobsledding is more of a match for its dangerous cousin, skeleton sledding.

Some things haven't changed too much: The runners beneath the sled are still made of steel. A jagged metal rod serves as the brake lever. The driver steers with a piece of rope in each hand, attached to a steering bolt below.

The most crucial element of the run is the beginning push, or lauf. It must combine power and timing to give the sled as fast a start as possible on the right line, and allow everyone to jump on board. Then it's up to the driver to take the best possible line, hugging the lip of each curve.

For the two-man competition, a sled can weigh more than 850 pounds with the athletes inside, and be almost nine feet long. For four-man bob, the total weight can be almost three-quarters of a ton (1,386 lbs.) and can be twelve and a half feet long. That's a lot of sled.

Jamaican Bobsledding: It's No Joke

For some people, their only impression of bobsledding came from the movie *Cool Runnings*, a comedy that loosely chronicled the story of the Jamaican bobsled team's journey to the 1988 Winter Olympics.

Nowadays, the Jamaican team is no joke. Its first Olympic competition garnered a 29th place finish in the two-man and a "Did Not Finish" in the four-man. They finished the 1994 Lillehammer competition in 14th, ahead of both American teams. Nagano, Japan, in 1998 was a slight disappointment as they slipped to 21st, but big things are expected in 2002.

Headed by Devon Harris, an original member of that 1988 team, the Jamaicans might even get a medal. In 2000, Jamaica's men's and women's teams won the world championships, a good sign that they will be competitive in Salt Lake City.

You may wonder: Where exactly does the Jamaican bobsled team practice? It's in Evanston, Wyoming, a small cowboy town that's a 30-minute drive from the Olympic Village in Utah. Team members deliver pizzas to help raise money for their Olympic bid. It isn't unusual for bobsledders to work day jobs to fundraise, but it isn't always the case. For example, Monaco's team has also been in Olympic competition in recent years, led by Albert Grimaldi. That's Prince Albert of Monaco, son of Prince Rainier and Princess Grace Kelly, and brother to Princess Caroline and Princess Stephanie. Prince Albert will also be in Utah in the two-man event, carrying on the tradition started by Kaiser Wilhelm of Germany. But celebrity sliders aren't limited to Europe's ruling elite.

Former NFL stars Willie Gault and Herschel Walker, as well as track star Edwin Moses, have all participated in the bobsled program. Only Walker actually competed in the Olympics (as a brakeman) and the days of celebrity sliders on Team USA are all but over. Nowadays, the U.S. Bobsled and Skeleton Federation recruits top athletes straight out of college, and they train for years.

Gourmet Pizza & Salads

SPECIALTY PIZZA Express™

FREE DELIVERY
CARRYOUT
(407) 869-0123

Open 7 days a week
LUNCH • DINNER • LATE-NIGHT
neighborhood SPECIALTY PIZZA EXPRESS is located behind Pebbles restaurant on 434, 1/4 mile West of I-4.

YES, I'M NUTS:
HOW DO I TAKE PART?

Well, you could call 1-800-BOBSLED or go to www.usbsf.com and try out for Team USA. Of course, you need to be in good physical condition, pass several tests, be in the Lake Placid region, pass more tests, join the U.S. Bobsled and Skeleton Federation, try out, and pass more tests.

If you happen to be near a bobsled run, you can take an afternoon off, pay a little bit of money, tour the site, get a lesson, and even ride with a professional.

IN THE RUNNING:
BOBBSLEDDERS TO WATCH

Here are some notables to watch as they shoot down the track like human bullets:

Jean Racine, U.S.A.: At just 22 years of age, Racine is the best female driver in the world and the easy Olympic favorite. A former junior luge and bob champion, Racine and partner Jen Davidson won five World Cup events in a row last year to finish second overall. Just 22, a rhyming name, and America's best shot at bobsled gold, all coming soon to a Wheaties box near you.

Francoise Burdet, Switzerland: This Swiss miss is Jean Racine's only real threat for her pursuit of Olympic Gold. She has consistently finished second or third behind Racine on the World Cup circuit and beat out Racine's sled by two one-hundredths of a second to win the 2001 World Championship event in Calgary and end Racine's five-event winning streak.

Todd Hays, U.S.A.: Recruited from the University of Tulsa, Hays is a former national kickboxing champion and college football player. He's the lead pilot on a rebuilding American team that hopes to get some respect in 2002. Hays competed at Nagano in 1998. We don't have to talk about where the team finished.

Christoph Langen, Germany: Keeping with the tradition of German dominance in the sport, Langen has been a dominant force in both two-man and four-man competitions for the past decade. Using German top-secret techniques and technology, Langen builds his own sleds. They're widely regarded as the fastest in the world. And he must be a pretty good driver, too. Langen won the World Championships in two-man and four-man in 2001, which was no surprise. He's the guy to beat at every bobsled competition.

Pierre Leuders, Canada: In the last 10 years, Leuders has taken 34 World Cup medals, 16 of them gold. He is the only man to win the World Cup two-man championships four times. With brakeman Dave MacEachern, Leuders won the gold at the 1998 Olympic Winter Games in Nagano.

NOTABLE SKELETON CRAZIES

Here's the buzz on who to watch at the Olympics:

Jim Shea, Jr., U.S.A.

You don't get a better pedigree than Jim Shea. His father and grandfather both competed in Winter Olympic events. Currently the top American, Shea was the first American to win a World Cup event in 1998. He won the World Cup the following year. Shea took home gold at the first Winter Goodwill Games in Lake Placid. He finished fourth at the 2001 World Championships in Calgary.

Juleigh Walker, U.S.A.

Walker is a pioneer in the sport. While competing on the men's national team, she was instrumental in strarting the women's team, winning women's national championships for 10 straight years, from 1990-99. She competed in the first international women's event and campaigned for women's bobsled and skeleton to be included in the 2002 Olympics.

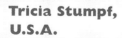

Tricia Stumpf, U.S.A.

Currently the top female slider on the American team, Stumpf won the 2001 World

Championship bronze medal on the Olympic course in Utah. She also won the 2000 U.S. Push Championships and looks poised to make a run at Olympic gold.

Lincoln DeWitt, U.S.A.

The world's best in 2001; winner of the World Cup after two bronzes, two silvers, and a gold medal-winning performance in Utah. DeWitt also won the North American Championships and owns records at the Olympic course in Park City, Utah.

Michelle Kelly, Canada

Young and blonde, she favors a one-piece lycra body suit. Combine that with her second-place finish for the 2000 World Cup, her records on the Calgary course, and Canada's strength as a team in women's skeleton, and she's sure to attract media attention.

Martin Burkhard, Republic of South Africa

Giving the Jamaican bobsled team a run for its money in the novelty department, Burkhard is vying to be the only Olympic skeleton slider from south of the equator.

Mertin Rettl, Austria

Look for red, purple, and blue hair underneath his helmet. This Austrian has been burning up the track of late, winning the 2001 World Championships and winning silver in Park City, Utah.

6
HIGH ENOUGH

Are you afraid of heights? It's actually a natural instinct. But if you want to overcome this fear, there's a way. These mountain sports are the perfect blend for Xtreme athletes who want the rush of being at high altitudes but also prefer to have their feet on solid ground (well, most of the time). And sometimes they scale heights for the simple pleasure of going back down at break-neck speeds on a mountain board or mountain bike.

Have you ever wondered what it takes to scale a rock like Tom Cruise in Mission: Impossible 2 (other than a stunt double and a huge net)? If that's not perilous enough, try climbing on ice. Yep, that's a sport, but, hey, there's no better way to keep warm than to keep moving. And do you want to find out just what the hell mountain boarding is? Keep reading.

ROCK CLIMBING/ ICE CLIMBING:
STONE COLD STUFF

On a sunny day as you hike along at your local park, you glance up and see a group of people high above you. As you squint, you notice someone clinging to the rock like Spiderman. Or maybe the image of Tom Cruise hanging by one hand off a precipice in *Mission: Impossible 2* fills you with a rush of adrenaline, and you want to brave the vertical adventure known as rock climbing. Or if that's not perilous enough, you can try climbing on ice, one of the most fun, exhilarating, and beautiful participation sports in the world, and at the same time one of the most dangerous. For some climbers, the act of clawing slowly up quaking blue pillars of frozen water becomes almost a spiritual quest. Either way, these are major highs.

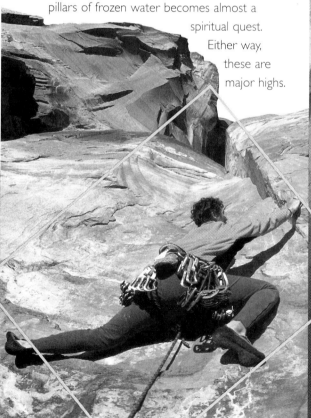

GET an INSTRUCTOR

Your first step to becoming a rock climber is to find someone to teach you. Do not try rock climbing alone. You need a partner for this sport, and you need someone to teach you the ropes. If you don't know any climbers, ask about climbing instruction at your local outdoor shop. They'll have brochures about local schools or organizations, or they may have instruction through the shop. Many serious climbers are fanatical about it: They love the sport and are eager to teach and convert newcomers, so they may invite you to join them immediately that day, that weekend, whenever you're ready to go.

Rock climbing has grown more popular in recent years—there are more than 350 climbing gyms in the U.S., and schools are popping up everywhere. Your school should be recognized by the American Mountain Guide Association; ask about its credentials and make sure you have a reputable instructor.

GRAB YOUR GEAR

You've got a trip lined up and a good teacher. Now you need to equip yourself with the right gear before you put yourself at the mercy of that fickle Mother Nature. Often you can rent the gear from the school, or if you've got a buddy who is an avid climber, he'll unearth some gear for you. You'll need shoes, a harness, chalk, ropes, carabiners, and other hardware to keep you hooked on to the rock and the ropes.

First you need to find yourself a snug-fitting shoe. Although you could climb in good tennis shoes, climbing shoes are specifically designed for rocks. They use a sticky rubber on the sole that molds better to

Your school should supply the rest of the equipment as part of the trip, so you don't need to rent or buy the ropes and hardware. Or if you're climbing with an experienced buddy, he's already got the goods. But you should learn the terms for the gear you'll be working with.

The ropes used in climbing are kernmantle lines. Similar to bungee cords, the ropes have a lot of give so that when you rest or fall, they bounce a little. You and the gear absorb less of the physical shock because of the elasticity of the ropes. (Unfortunately, there's no gear to absorb any emotional shock.)

To keep your hands from sweating, you grab chalk (magnesium carbonate) from a bag hooked to your harness; it's the same stuff that gymnasts use. Remember that you can grip the rock better when you keep your hands dry. If your hands are sweaty, they get slippery and that's not good. (Also note that you don't climb in the rain because you can't grip the rock well.)

Carabiners are oval or d-shaped metal devices that hold the rope. You should use only UIAW-approved carabiners. Don't even think about using similar-looking devices from a hardware store—they will break under the stress of human weight. Carabiners attach to anchors that climbers bolt into the rock.

the rock surface. As you might expect, having a good grip on the rock is critical. Duh. A harness is a nylon contraption that you wear around your waist and legs; it bears your weight when you fall or rest. It is sometimes dubbed a basket or a diaper (you figure that last term out). If you borrow or rent the harness, give it a good once-over; check that it is not frayed or discolored. You might also want to take a whiff to check that the harness doesn't smell rancid from being stored improperly. You want a harness that's in good condition, otherwise it may not suffer your weight. Fraying, discoloration, or a bad smell warn you that a harness is not fit for use.

ROCK ON

You're ready to go with your instructor, and you've got your gear, so it's time to get on the rock. The first time you climb you will be top-roping, which means you use a rope that threads through an anchor so the rope and anchor form a pulley system. The climber who places the hardware and the rope is lead climbing; there is no top rope for her to use as a pulley, instead she relies on a system in which her rope threads through anchors she places as she climbs. Because she is the first to go up she is "sending it."

Don't worry, you will not send it for a while. When you top-rope, the climbing rope threads through the top anchor, and you knot it to a loop or hardware on your harness. Your partner will take up the other end of the rope and keep it taut or feed you slack as you climb; this is called belaying.

Check that your harness is secure. Make sure that the tail of the waist belt is passed back through the buckle (it goes through once and then you loop it back), and that all tails—those on the waist belt and on the leg straps—are all tucked in. You don't want any loose ends that could snag on the rock. Wear clothes that won't bind you—they should be loose enough not to inhibit your movement, but not too loose. You've got to see your feet while you climb so that you can find footholds. Some newbie climbers go up the rock with wide-legged pants and fall a lot because they can't see

where they're putting their feet. Also your clothing should fit the temperature; wear something that you don't need to take off if it gets too hot.

Before you get on the rock, scan the surface and find your route. You want some idea of where you plan to go before you try hauling yourself up an unknown element. After you pick out your route, you need to let your partner know that you're ready. Communicating well and often with your partner is essential to safe climbing.

You say, "On belay?" and she'll answer, "Belay's on," if she is ready. Basically, you're just saying, "I'm ready; are you ready?" and she's saying, "Yeah." Then you get on the rock and start climbing.

CLIMBING STYLE

When you climb you want to work efficiently so that you don't expend all of your energy and get "pumped." Pumped is a term climbers use when lactic acid builds up in their arms, and they can't hold on any

more. (If you're a beginner, and you're pumped, then you're probably gripped, too, which means you're scared out of your mind.)

Since you're hanging off of a rock, you might think you need strong arms. But you should be climbing with your legs. Obviously, as you get more advanced, you may find yourself hanging on by two fingers and a toe. In those cases, strong fingers and arms are advantageous, but in the beginning you want to rely on the big muscles in your thighs.

slack." Your belayer will hold the rope taut so that the harness supports your weight. You also yell "Take," if you think you're going to fall. Shrieking, "I'm falling!" will also do the trick.

Now you may wonder how you get back down once you've scaled a rock face. Rappelling is the process of slowly hopping back down the rock as your belayer releases more slack on the rope. You place yourself in a stance in which you are nearly perpendicular to the rock. Often new climbers get

Avoid flattening yourself against the surface. Though it's tempting to huddle against the rock like it's your mama, you need to keep your chest away from the rock. Again, when you are away from the rock you put the bulk of your weight on your legs. You also have a better view of the path ahead. Always keep at least three points of contact with the rock (two legs and one arm or two arms and one leg).

As you climb, your partner may keep the rope slack, so that you can move easily. If you feel you need a rest, you can say, "Take," which means "Take up the

overzealous or a little frightened when they rappel back down. Use caution because you can hurt yourself if you go too fast or don't maintain good form. For example, if you don't stay perpendicular, you are more likely to crash into the rock. Just take your time and take it slow.

RATING THE ROCK

You may want to know how your route is rated when you climb it. Rock climbing uses a specific rating system to define the difficulty of a route. The American

rating system is the Yosemite Decimal System (YDS), which grew out of a system introduced in 1937 as the Sierra Club system. Terrain is categorized into different classes ranging from Class 1 for hiking up to Class 5 for rock climbing that requires technical gear.

The rates for rock climbing range between 5.0 and 5.14+, and the rate that a slope receives is defined by the hardest move on the route. Most novice climbers start on rocks that rate between 5.0-5.7, while weekend climbers are comfy on 5.8 and 5.9 grades. You see only dedicated climbers on rocks that rate at 5.10 and above. Knowing the rating for your climb helps you talk with other climbers, and, let's admit it: It can give you bragging rights when you explain it to the vertically challenged.

SEND IT

The key to becoming a good climber, as with most skills, is to gain confidence and climb often. If you can find a regular climbing partner, you're lucky. You can learn each other's habits and build up a good rapport. Remember that good communication is essential for safe climbing, and you learn and improve when you have a regular partner.

ICE IT

A blanket of snow lies glistening in the sun. The long morning shadows stretch 200 feet below as you hold on to your precarious perch. "Ice," you shout, as a refrigerator-sized block of a frozen waterfall knocked loose by your ice pick drops. "Ice! Ice! Ice!" you shout louder as it falls until, "whump," a snow drift becomes a swirling tornado of white, just missing your partner, who shouts up to you. "Daaaaaammmmm! That was a friggin' huge block."

You look down to see him grinning madly and covered with the fine powder fallout of the bomb you dropped near him.

"Okay?" you shout.

"Sure, just stop throwing chunks at me," comes the reply. "That ice is sketchy."

Ice climbers see nature in a way that few people ever do. They are usually up before sunrise. They then spend the whole day, or maybe more, in remote, snow covered places where crowds of people never go. They put themselves in dangerous situations; help could be days away. Ice climbers find themselves hanging from a block of ice, arms tired, legs trembling, while trying to drill in a stubborn ice screw that will just not bite. And until this harrowing moment passes, either with their successfully climbing the section, or taking a 30-foot, 40-foot, or who knows how long a fall, their fate very much hangs in the balance. Plus it's cold.

GEAR

To climb ice, you will need a big pile of gear. This gear is expensive and specialized. It will do you very little good anywhere else—it's for ice climbing, and, with the exception of rock climbing or cat-burglary, has no other purpose. Some common sense ice climbing advice: Don't buy anything until you are really sure you like to ice climb. There are many mountaineering and gear shops, as well as guide services, that will rent you the gear for ice climbing. This is the way to go, because once you commit, it will cost $1,200 to $2,000 for equipment.

While it is expensive in terms of an initial investment in equipment, the sport otherwise is virtually free—almost every ice climb in the world, with a few notable exceptions, is open for anyone to try and your gear will last for years.

Every piece of ice climbing gear has a simple and obvious purpose.
Axes are

quite straightforward: They are about two feet long, with an alloy or carbon-fiber handle and a sharp pick straight out of a bad horror movie. The crampons that fit on the end of your boots and that are used for gripping the ice look like little bear traps; the boots look like, well, boots. Other gear usually consists of two ropes or one twin rope, a helmet, five to 10 ice screws (an eight-inch long, inch-and-a half in diameter, threaded hollow tube) to attach the rope to the ice, about 10 nylon slings, around 20 caribiners (an aluminum snap link used to attach the rope to the screw), and sunglasses. Apart from this safety gear, most ice climbers opt for things like Gore-Tex gloves, jackets, or pants, high quality long underwear, good backpacks, stoves, and back rests. For most beginners, these are the last items that should be bought. A simple pair of wool pants, long underwear, a sweater, hat, and gloves will keep most folks plenty warm as they are starting out.

To learn how to climb ice without killing yourself, you will probably need to take at least one class, much as you do in rock climbing. In the class, you should learn how to set up top ropes, attach the gear to your body, and ascend ice with the aid of ice-climbing picks and crampons. If you opt to take a class, be sure to ask if you will learn to set up top ropes. This is critically important for you to become a self-sufficient ice climber, as it will permit you to set up a rope system in which the rope goes from the ground up to the top of the climb, then back down to the climber. The ropes are held with the ice screws. It is a safe way to learn the techniques of ice climbing.

The first time you ice climb, if you have never rock climbed, you will need to learn how to belay. The belay is a way to control the rope while your partner climbs. One of several devices will be attached to your harness to apply friction to the rope in case of a fall. It's important to remember when you belay to never let go of the rope. Generally, when you belay, the left hand reels in the rope to keep the tension as the climber heads up the ice while the right hand pulls the rope through the belay device. The right hand is the "brake" hand, so if a climber falls, the rope is bent and stops the fall. It's important to act quickly to shorten the fall as much as possible. When your partner is climbing, his life is in your hands.

When you first climb, you will be on a top rope. This technique, described above, makes it virtually impossible to fall. While on a top rope, it is okay to sit and rest in your harness, suspended by the rope. Don't get used to hanging, because when you start to lead climb, you will have little, if any, opportunity for rest.

Another way to get your feet wet (or more accurately, frozen) in ice climbing is to tag along with some experienced ice climbers. This works well if you already know how to rock climb and can handle the rope work with little instruction. It also works well if you have patient friends who ice climb. The problem is that not that many ice climbers are known for their unending patience. Yet, if you are polite and eager to learn, finding a willing teacher shouldn't be too hard.

To find someone to take you out, spend some time at a sport-climbing gym or bouldering area or a bar, anywhere climbers frequent. Look for the antisocial, scruffy individuals with big calves and more bulky bodies than sport climbers. There is a fairly good chance that, if they are ice climbers, you will be able to convince them, with a six pack or two, to take you along.

INDOOR CLIMBING

You can also get started with climbing at a gym that has an indoor climbing wall. Usually, you must sign up for a basic class before you can get on the wall. Just as with outdoor climbing, you need a partner when you climb on an indoor wall. Go with a friend, or ask whether the staff at the gym will work with you.

For indoor climbing at a gym, you will need shoes and a harness, which you can rent. The ropes are already attached to the walls. Routes are usually color-coded based on difficulty, and the staff will explain which colors coordinate with easier routes. Indoor climbing is a great way to improve your climbing skills; you can practice, get stronger, and stay warm.

MOUNTAIN BIKING

Everyone knows how to ride a bike, right? Piece of cake. But when it comes to riding off road on two wheels, be prepared for something different. And a few bumps and bruises later, you, too, could be saying things like, "Dude, I tried a tabletop on my old school hardtail and drew first blood when I endoed—I'm stoked I was wearing a lid!"

THERE'S A HISTORY?

There is an ongoing debate in the cycling community about the roots of mountain biking. Most consider Marin County, California, the home of the fat tire. Just beyond San Francisco's Golden Gate Bridge, legend has it, the locals rigged up road bikes and attempted adrenaline-pumping descents down Mount Tamalpais' steep fire roads in the 1970s.

Shortly after, companies—Gary Fischer's for one—put knobby tires on ten-speeds with upright handlebars, and started making bikes that combined the best aspects of BMX bikes and racing bikes. These early mountain bikes were heavy, clunky, and expensive, but they opened up the off-road world to a horde of disgruntled suburbanites yearning for freedom.

IT HURTS SO GOOD

Responding to demand for bikes that offer more than the Sears 10-speed of yesteryear, bike manufacturers like Giant, Trek, and Cannondale have pushed affordable rides into stores. Commercials have pumped images of shiny tanned models loading Treks onto roof racks, and events like the X Games and the Olympics have showcased mountain biking to the masses.

But don't start sweating just yet, you don't need the expensive Trek and the roof rack. And you don't have to be tan and training for the X Games to enjoy mountain biking. The fun lies in the adventure and exploration, the rush of the trees flying by, the rocks that you'll hammer over, the river crossing that you'll

grind through. Nothing can compare to the majestic scenery that you'll find when you venture out into the mountains, woods, or desert. Forget about your bike and whether it is or isn't some *unobtanium* (defined as some expensive "unobtainable" bike material) and think about where you are and what you are doing. Once that becomes evident, the fun is almost as endless as the single track and just about as cheap. Your heart will charge and your eyes will widen while you struggle to stay on your bike. The rocks will grab at your tires as if starving for a piece of your exposed flesh.

READY, SET, GO GET A CLUE (THE 411)

As a beginner you'll most likely be riding a bike that is not being featured in one of the flashy newsstand magazines. So what? Find a bike that fits your budget. Best adjust your bike to your body, as it's easier than trying to grow longer legs or shortening your spine. There are many metals and composites that make up frames these days. Bang for the buck, aluminum is the way to go. Light, stiff, and relatively cheap, there will be plenty of bikes to choose from. Spend some coin on an entry-level front suspension fork. It will allow you to ride stronger and longer, sucking up bumps, saving you energy, and making your ride much more entertaining. Forget the rear suspension for now. It can be costly and gimmicky and can make your bike feel like a Cadillac—smooth on the flats, but like a tank on the climbs and a mobile home through any tight single track (a narrow trail for bikes).

Another consideration: clipless pedals. All the racers are using them, so you know they must be the move. Easier to handle than you think, clipless pedals have a mechanism that allows the rider to click special ATB shoes (All Terrain Bicycle) into the pedal, thus improving the pedal

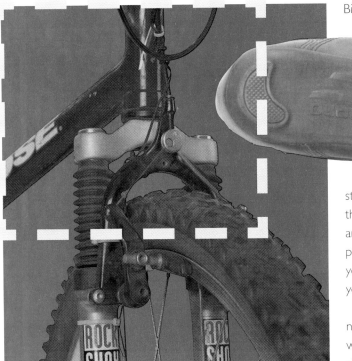

stroke and energy output. Before you take to the trail with them, go to an empty parking lot and practice clipping in and out of the pedals by pushing down on the toe to get in and turning your heel away from the bike to get out. Before you know it you'll be locked in and cruising.

Perhaps the most important thing you will need will be your lid—the helmet. Riding without one means you're an idiot, plain and simple. That is unless you have plans on

make baggy shorts with the chamois padded crotch so your privates are protected, and you can look slick even on the trail.

There are endless ways to carry water, from bottle mounts to hydration backpacks. Most packs can be fitted with pockets and pouches to carry just about anything you can think of. Once you get an idea of what type of terrain you'll be riding, then go make the purchase. But you might ask yourself: Why buy the 1740 cubic inch CamelBak Trans Alp Hydration Backpack with suspension harness and internal cargo organizer when all you really do is spin for 45 minutes on the local trails after work or school? A water bottle and a Snickers stashed in a jersey pocket will do the trick.

NOW STOP POSING AND START PEDDLING

You roll up to the trail with your shiny new bike, baggy shorts all chill, and legs flexed. The locals, both the boys and the Bettys, stammer, "Who's the new jack with the monster thighs? Damn!" You may look like Lance Armstrong, but you probably ride like Stretch Armstrong. What they don't know is that the new jack doesn't know jack either. But that's okay, you can fix that.

becoming an organ donor. Everyone rides with one from your grandma to pro racers. It is the law in most places, and if you show up to the trailhead without one you might get a verbal smackdown from some of the locals. With so many new brands, designs, and choices, you'll find one that matches your tastes and head size. Make sure it sits forward, not back, on your noggin and fits snug when you ride.

Other considerations are clothes and how you want to carry your spare tubes, tools, and water. Padded bike shorts do make a difference. They

Good Manners

Cyclists are super friendly folk as long as you know trail etiquette. For example, give those coming up the same trail in the other direction the right of way. It is much easier to stop and then start again when going downhill. Like your mom waxed, respect others and they will respect you. Remember that most of the best trails are located in multi-use land areas. Hiking, bird watching, and horseback riding are all usually allowed on the same terrain you might be barreling through.

Watch where you go, stay on the trail, and be humble. Across the country, mountain bike advocacy groups have worked hard to open up access to trails for mountain bike riders. If you hack off enough hikers and park rangers with loud and obnoxious language, out of control riding, and the littering of Cliff Bar wrappers, you may find that the killer single track that you used to covet is no longer open to you or anybody on two wheels. Like it or not, your behavior and attitude impact the reputation as well as the riding of all mountain bikers. With that being said, get outside, be safe, ride smart, and you will have a blast.

The best place to learn mountain biking technique is on easy terrain. Practice on pavement and then dirt roads before heading to any single track. These open and flat spaces will allow you to adjust the seat height, loosen your pedals, test out your suspension, and more important, learn how to shift. Because much of the best terrain is varied and steep, the rider must always learn which shifters change which gears. Almost all stock-shop bikes come with gripshifts, making it easy to run through your cog set (the set of chain rings your chain goes over), from small to big, with a twist of the wrist. But if you don't know which way to turn your wrist, you could be powering in to your smallest cog and, therefore, hardest gear to pedal when you approach a climb. What does this mean? You'll be stopped dead in your tracks, torque a knee, get passed by Mr. McSweeney, your 56-year-old retired school bus driver on his sweet titanium hog, and end up walking your bike to the top of the hill. In other words, learn to shift before you hit the trails.

There are some other skills that you can pick up in the parking lot that will save you from picking up pieces of yourself up on the trail. Learn to get over small obstacles like a curb, or those concrete things that mark parking spaces. This is one of the most important skills that you can learn, because all things extreme depend on the basic principles you'll learn doing this. The similarities between those concrete things and a downed tree limb are pretty amazing. There are basically three ways to get over obstacles. The first and easiest is to just ride over the obstacle. This is also the most likely to split your noggin open, too. The best case scenario is that the front wheel will just pop up in the air a bit,

and the rear wheel will bump over it, and you'll be safely on the other side. Here's what can go wrong: If the log or whatever is too big for you to get over, your front wheel will stop dead, but you will not. Since your feet will still be attached to the bike, you'll do a face plant, and the bike will land on top of you. At least you'll be on the other side of the log, and hey, now you know what an endo is. Oh, and you might ruin your front wheel. There's nothing more embarrassing than carrying your pretzeled-front-wheel-bike out of the woods with a broken nose. That is why the other two methods are worth learning.

The first of these two is the technical solution, which is best used when you're already moving slowly, like up a steep hill, or when the obstacle is in a potentially dangerous location (like next to a cliff face). (Technical just means it requires some skill to get right.) You drop your gear down so that you're moving slowly

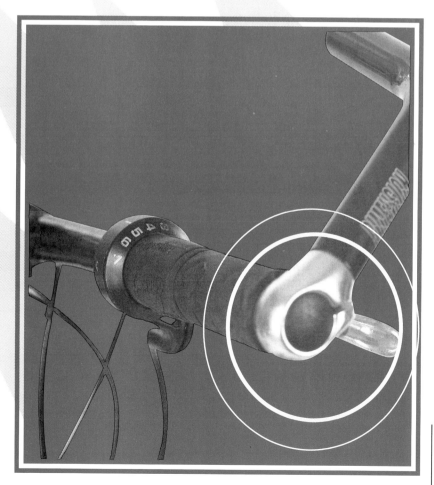

but still have some pedal RPMs. As your front wheel approaches the obstacle, get your butt out of the saddle, move your shoulders back, put your weight back, and pull up and back on the handle bars. It should feel like you're doing a row at the gym. This will get the front wheel off of the ground. We used to call it a wheelie when we were kids. You want the wheel to just get high enough to clear the obstacle, then let it roll over the top. Once the front wheel is up (and/or over)

shift your weight forward, and the back wheel will follow over fairly easily. If you're in a very short gear, you may be able to assist the back wheel with some pedaling. Once you get good at this, you'll hardly have to slow down to pull it off. There is even a variation on this for getting over things that are higher than the bottom of the chain ring (that's the spikey part next to the

pedals). You just let the chain ring spin over the obstacle the same way the back wheel would. It is possible to get over a two-foot or greater diameter fallen tree like this. Be careful, though, you can bend a chain ring this way, and there are products like the "rock-ring" that are designed specifically to guard your chain ring in situations like this.

The second recommended method is the bunny hop. Mechanically, a bunny hop is fairly similar to an ollie on a skateboard. By throwing your weight down, then using the compression to generate spring and leaping with the bike, you can get both wheels off the ground at the same time, even at a virtual standstill. If you're moving, and are clipped into the pedals, you can get some serious air. Just use your strong foot to give the bike a quick thrust of forward energy, and crouch and lift up on the handlebars at the same time to get the front wheel in the air (not too high, though). When the wheel is at the desired height, quickly spring up and shift your weight up and forward to lift the back wheel. Try this with small objects at low speed first. The easiest thing to do is to hop on and off of curbs until you get good at it. Also, be prepared to crash a couple of times while you're learning. Hey, you might not, but don't say we didn't warn you. Once you have mastered the bunny hop, you'll be bombing the hills and catching mad air over anything in your way.

There's one more thing to learn before you hit the trail. Learn to ride slowly. Moving slow and threading a needle with your front tire is one of the most difficult things you can learn to do, but when you're fighting up a 15 degree grade that's strewn with head-sized boulders, you'll be glad you spent the time. Unless you can weave your way through those kinds of obstacles, and have the right balance of technique and strength, you'll have to face the ultimate humiliation of having to get off the bike. And the only way to get good at it is to practice. But if you keep at it, you'll be doing wheel stands and turning like the hand on a clock in no time. Ride slowly, pay attention to your balance, and plan ahead, and you too can be the baddest techno-weenie on the trail.

BREAK
LIKE THE WIND

Now that you have the skills and the looks to go along, stop messing around and head to some single track. Mountain bike riders live for this stuff and now you will find out why. Riding through trees along ridges and over rocks on a thin line of dirt is what your bike was designed to do.

Here is where the subtleties of balance, power, and bike handling will be showcased. The basics are simple: When climbing, stay seated and drop your elbows. Your body weight will keep your rear wheel from slipping. Your elbows help put more of your torso over the top tube by preventing your front wheel from popping up. For descents, get up and out of the saddle and have your weight back. Keep on the

balls of your feet and your knees bent for balance and shock absorption. Always have two fingers on the break levers and realize that your front break has 60 percent more stopping power. What does that mean? If you need to stop quickly, the front brake has more force. However, if you brake too strong with your weight forward, things can get ugly—like doing a front flip over the handlebars.

That is why many new riders look for instruction. Now more than ever you can learn from the best almost anywhere in the country and throughout the world. There are famous schools in mountain bike meccas like Moab, Utah; Crested Butte, Colorado; and Mt. Snow, Vermont.

Tours and camps are popping up everywhere from upstate New York to Quito, Ecuador, led by local trail gurus to seasoned racers. Numerous ski resorts bring in much needed revenue when the snow isn't falling by opening the trails and lifts to mountain bikers. Most also rent some killer bikes and have staff who teach riding classes from beginner to expert. You can contact any local shop in your area or NORBA (National Off Road Bicycle Association) for your specific needs or questions about where to find instruction.

Once you get comfortable on your steed and learn some riding technique, don't book plane tickets to Moab just yet. Practice on the local trails until you have them dialed. Know each corner, all the hills and every rock. Be able to shift effortlessly, gliding from eye-popping drops, up and over the rollers, and through the flats. Learn how to adjust your bike's brakes and seat post and learn how to fix a flat. Get a system down in which you know what to bring on each ride (i.e., tools, extra clothing, spare tubes, energy bars, and water). Take to the trails with experienced people, watching how they corner and pedal. This is perhaps the best and cheapest way to get fast quickly.

MOUNTAIN BOARDING: ALL-TERRAIN, ALL THE TIME

Like many newer Xtreme sports, mountain boarding can trace its genesis to the need for speed, but a big part of the attraction for mountain boarders is *where* they find the action. Racing down mountain slopes, these all-terrain boarders dodge boulders and trees, leave flying pebbles, and create clouds of dust in their wake.

No longer dependent on fickle snowfalls and high-priced lift tickets for thrills, they've slipped the bonds of single-season fun. Boards aren't cheap, but once purchased they can go virtually anywhere at any time—and at no additional cost.

DESIGN INNOVATIONS

Manufacturers continually make design innovations, using composite materials, and including brakes and steering mechanisms. Taking a cue from mountain bikes, many board makers incorporate shock-absorbing suspensions. Also like mountain bikes, most wheel designs feature pneumatic (air-filled) tires. An exception: Models marketed by the Xtreme Wheelz Corporation feature solid latex tires that won't go flat.

In the Beginning

Most insiders agree that mountain boards (also known as all-terrain boards) have been around in one form or another since the 1970s. One early manufacturer, the Xtreme Wheelz Corporation, produced a skateboard with modified wheels for off-road use in the 1980s. But it was not until the early 1990s that a frustrated surfer and two snowboarders, living in two different hemispheres, independently hit on ideas that would take off-road boarding to a new level. These pioneers began toying with modifications aimed at re-creating the feel of surfing and snowboarding.

In 1992, Jason Lee and Patrick McConnell—two frustrated snowboarders looking for warm season thrills and a viable business idea—came up with early board designs that intrigued local snowboarders and skateboarders. Says Lee, "We combined the frame and deck in one piece, allowing for more vertical suspension."

Clamoring for samples, neighborhood athletes helped popularize the new sport, which soon became known as mountain boarding. In 1993, Lee and McConnell formed a company (MBS Mountainboards, LLC) and interest in their unusual product snowballed quickly.

At about the same time, Australian surfer John Milne created his own version of the all-terrain board in an attempt to recreate the experience of surfing on dry land. Frustrated with days when the waves were too calm to surf, he was searching for a land-based alternative to the sport he loved. He came up with a board using two front wheels and one centrally mounted rear wheel for stability through turns. His early three-wheel board impressed California entrepreneur Jim Katzaroff, who with his brother purchased the worldwide marketing rights to the product from Milne, and founded Outback Mountainboards in the United States.

In the intervening years since MBS and Outback introduced their first groundbreaking models, at least 25 competing manufacturers have sprung up around the globe. According to The Wall Street Journal, more than one million all-terrain boarders had snapped up boards and taken to the dirt in search of off-road fun by 1998. As Lee and McConnell had hoped, their clever invention gave rise to one of the fastest growing sports in an increasingly crowded field of Xtreme sports. Even with the number of mountain board owners at the one million milestone, the sport is still in its infancy. It continues to catch on with mountain bikers, surfers, in-line skaters, skateboarders, skiers, snowboarders, and other adrenaline junkies, and shows no sign of losing speed.

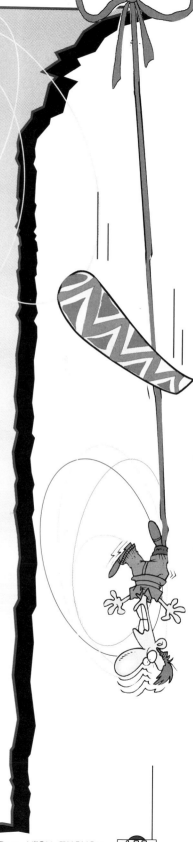

Wheel configurations vary greatly, ranging from four conventionally mounted tires (the most common arrangement), to three, six, or eight wheels in various configurations. One innovator from Australia offers an in-line, two-wheeled board with relatively large-diameter wheels, which resembles a bicycle with no seat or handlebars. Manufacturers market tires for general and specific uses, including for use exclusively on sand or grass, but most boards are intended for general off-road use. Like mountain bike tires, the tires on all-terrain boards are generally fat and nubby, the better to grip rough, bumpy, often-loose surfaces.

Some boards feature a hand-activated brake cable, much like the brakes on a mountain bike. Discs mounted on the insides of wheel hubs provide the friction necessary to stop fast. Other designs use a foot-activated brake pedal at the back of the board. Some manufacturers recommend adjusting tire inflation pressure based on skill level. Lower pressures are recommended for beginners, so the ride will be somewhat slower and smoother.

Today's boards combine elements borrowed from snowboards, mountain bikes, skateboards, and even surfboards to provide a platform that will sail over virtually any surface, in any weather, at any time.

Some hybrid sports have been developed based on the all-terrain board platform, making use of a sail, either hand-held or mast mounted, for land-based boardsailing. Another ingenious modification makes use of a kite for wind-powered flight across land.

YOU CAN DO IT, TOO

Hawaiian native Akoni Kama has been mountain boarding for more than six years. "It's like the last great board sport," says Kama, who is also a spokesman for Outback Mountainboards. Kama grew up surfing Oahu's famous breakers, and he's involved in all kinds of board sports. But he was especially attracted to mountain boarding, which allows him to "surf" on days when the ocean's surf isn't up to his standard. Says Kama, "You can ride the street, the dirt, the mountains." In fact, it seems there's virtually nowhere a determined mountain boarder can't go. Kama has made a hair-raising descent of an Alaskan glacier on a mountain board, skirting a crevasse the entire way.

FIRST STEPS

It's smart to suit up with plenty of protective gear, including a helmet, elbow and kneepads, gloves or wrist guards. You'll need to find a suitable place for your maiden voyage, such as a gentle grass slope with a "big roll-out," which means plenty of level space at the bottom (without obstructions) where you can coast to a stop, if necessary. Ideally, you should avoid hills with trees, rocks, or other obstacles. If you're especially afraid of crashing, invest in a board with a hand or foot-operated brake. For beginners, a hand brake may feel more comfortable, while experienced riders tend to prefer the freedom of a heel-operated brake.

LEARNING TO STOP

"First, test your brakes," is the mountain board mantra. Once you've learned to stop with confidence, you will be ready to let fly. But remember that you can't stop on a dime. It's more like a car, which becomes especially important if you do any street riding.

After you're comfortable riding your board down gentle 20- to 30-foot slopes, try climbing a little higher, or move on to a slightly steeper slope. Remember to keep your knees bent, and use your arms for balance. Once you become accustomed to descending gentle slopes and operating your brake effectively, you'll be ready to graduate to more challenging surfaces such as dirt-covered slopes, or the street. The beauty of a mountain board is that you're not restricted to pavement. Your board can go from street, to yard, to mountaintop and back, with ease—okay, relative ease.

CARVE CONTROL

Carving turns snowboard-style allows a boarder to control speed. Done properly, they are a graceful and natural way to descend a slope. Done by you, they are an experiment in terror.

Begin by carving wide turns on gentle slopes, like a beginning skier descending in broad, slow turns down the bunny slope. If you gain too much speed, use your brake to regain control. As your turns improve, begin making tighter ones. Keep your knees bent as you turn, leaning slightly uphill and keeping your weight centered over the board. If the board begins sliding out from under you in a turn, you're probably going too fast, and need to apply the brakes. Go into your deepest crouch while actually carving the arc of the turn, and gently rise through the downhill portion of your descent. Stay relaxed, but alert.

For STARTERS

To get started in mountain boarding, the pros recommend investing in a balance board—a simple oval board with a separate cylindrical roller that's about the size of a large aerosol can. This balance-training aid is available in stores or online (one site is www.indoboard.com) for about $100. Named for its usefulness indoors, the indoboard allows athletes to prepare for challenges that will be encountered outdoors, where the potential for noggin bumps are greater.

POWER SLIDE

Finally, as your skills improve you'll probably want to learn the power slide, a stopping technique that requires no brakes. It resembles a hockey skater's sliding stop on ice. Begin as if carving a turn, but instead of turning your board back downhill, keep it perpendicular to the fall line. With your knees bent, reach down and grab your outside (downhill) rail (the board's edge). Lean toward the inside (uphill) rail and stay centered over the board until you slide to a stop. Practice until you're able to snap into a slide and skid to a stop with ease. Eventually, you will no longer need to grip the outside rail during the turn. Rather, you will use your arms for balance. Remember to lean uphill, or you could pitch forward and stop on your head rather than your feet.

GAINING ACCEPTANCE

Somebody has to set the rules, even in mountain boarding. In 1994, the All-Terrain Boarding Association (ATBA) was set up as the sport's governing body.

The organization's goal is to standardize competition, promote the sport, and address safety issues. ATBA recognizes two distinct forms of all-terrain or mountain boarding competition: racing and freestyle. The emphasis is obviously on speed in the former, and on (increasingly sophisticated and spectacular) stunts in the latter. Freestyle competitions are subdivided further into several categories. In "big air," boarders are judged on the difficulty of their chosen tricks, their individual style, the height they attain, and the degree to which they smoothly stick their landings. Top competitors complete spectacular spinning jumps and inverted aerial maneuvers, just as in skateboarding and snowboarding. In "slope style" competition, riders attempt successive freestyle jumps, which are judged according to

criteria similar to those used in big air competitions. A final competition involves distance jumping.

Riders who race compete in a head-to-head format on BMX-style courses. They feature dirt berms, obstacles, and jumps, and can be constructed on ski slopes or open downhill areas. Dual or giant slalom pits two boarders against each other. Competitors must go through successive gates and complete required jumps and other moves. In street-X, riders compete head-to-head in a fast-paced free-for-all competition that may feature jumps and other obstacles.

7

ADVENTURE RACING: CAN YOU SURVIVE?

For nearly a decade, intrepid teams from more than 20 countries have braved the wilderness and competed against each other in what many consider the toughest expedition race in the world. It's called the Eco-Challenge, and it takes place in remote settings such as Borneo and the Australian outback. It attracts a huge television audience (more than 144 million viewers worldwide), as well as "celebrity teams" (Playboy magazine sent an all-female squad), not to mention triggering some damn strange injuries. For example, participant Dave Hulme had a leech crawl up his penis. The cure? Not amputation, thank God—he just drank a lot of water. Whatever, millions marvel as teams struggle through a race that pits endurance and courage against about the worst nature has to offer. In fact, the challenge is produced by Mark Burnett, the guy who came up with the television smash, Survivor.

TEAMWORK

Basically the Eco-Challenge has four-member teams (which must include at least one woman) who trek across hundreds of miles of terrain for six to 10 days. Their travel modes range from kayaking whitewater to climbing up mountains, and, to win, the team must complete the entire course together. Teams are expected to be self-sufficient; they must supply their own food and medical supplies, repair their own equipment, and choose their own route without outside support.

ECO-CHALLENGE:
Surviving the Worst, 1995-2000

To *Survivor* enthusiasts, it should come as no surprise that Mark Burnett, the mastermind behind the mega-popular reality television show, is also responsible for bringing us the Eco-Challenge. He seems to have an obsession with the idea of Man vs. Nature.

Upon viewing European endurance races and New Zealand-based multi-sport challenges, he thought what any mega-minded bigshot would think, "I can make that better!"

More than just your average corporate suit, though, Burnett doesn't mind getting his own hands dirty in order to understand what really goes on. He recruited an American team (and named himself captain) to compete in a European race. Bringing the U.S. its first top ten finish in these competitions, he felt he had an understanding of the event, and began

planning what would become the first Eco-Challenge, which was held in 1995 in Utah.

Burnett decided to make the race tougher by eliminating assistance crews that were prevalent in the European races, forcing teams to be more self-sufficient. In the Utah race, contestants trekked over land and water, starting out on foot and horseback to a canyon, where they then had to navigate a river, negotiate narrow passages, and climb over slippery ledges.

The next stage was trekking through the desert, first on foot, then with the aid of mountain bikes. By this point, several teams dropped out of the race. After that, the remaining teams faced a rigorous mountain course. Rappelling, climbing over more ledges, and navigating long bridges finally brought members to the valley floor, where they then trekked toward the

whitewater rafting test.

They faced over 20 rapids up to Class V (the nastiest kinds) during the 52-mile water expedition; many teams flipped their rafts and were forced to swim the foamy waters. Then it really got tough. The teams hit a 1,200-foot canyon wall they had to climb. (Starting to get the picture?) This led them to another water leg, a 50-plus mile stretch of Lake Powell they had to paddle in canoes to the finish line.

The U.S. had a dismal showing in that competition. Out of 50 teams, 38 raced under the American banner, and only one U.S. team (Benincasa/Nike/ACG) finished in the top five.

The second Eco-Challenge, held later in 1995, moved across America to New England, spanning through the states of Maine and Rhode Island. Only 12 teams were up to the standards of this competition and, of those, only eight were able to finish the 320-mile course.

Picking up right where the previous race left off,

this one began with teams canoeing through 93 miles of lakes, rivers, and ponds. From there, the competitors rafted through a 12-mile whitewater cavern. Teams then had to give up their rafts in favor of hiking boots as they navigated through thick forests and dangerous bogs on their way to fixed ropes where they had to make a grueling climb up overhanging cliff faces.

The last legs of the course involved mountain biking through a single track strewn with logs, rocks, tree stumps, plus a river crossing, then they were flown to Martha's Vineyard (giving them a few precious moments of rest), where the teams kayaked across nearly 70 miles of ocean to the finish line in Newport, Rhode Island.

The next year (1996), the Eco-Challenge opted for a change of climate (worse, naturally) traveling to the province of British Columbia in Canada. The cold weather added to the difficulty of the competition, introducing the thrill of glacier trekking. The cold, no doubt, did its job: Only 14 of 70 teams completed the course.

In 1997, Burnett and crew finally took the Eco-Challenge off of the North American continent, jetting to the outback of Australia. The challenges were right on par with those in the previous races, including trekking through the wilderness, mountain biking, ropes courses, whitewater rafting, canoeing, and kayaking, but the Australian outback added a new danger—wildlife, in the form of insects, plants, and wild animals.

The teams faced such perils as spiders, extremely poisonous snakes, poisonous plants, and, of course, the dreaded crocodiles. The contestants persevered, however, and out of 48 teams, 29 finished with all members alive, with Team Eco-Internet coming in first with a race time of 5 days, 19 hours, and 46 minutes.

In 1998 the race moved up to Morocco, challenging the competitors with camel rides and navigating part of the African coastline, along with challenge staples, such as mountain biking, rappelling, kayaking, and mountaineering. Team Vail crossed the finish line at 6 days, 22 hours, and 15 minutes to bring victory to the United States.

Adventure seekers then converged south of the equator once again, in Argentina in 1999. In this race, 51 teams kayaked, rode horseback, and rappelled over diverse terrain ranging from grasslands to glaciers, with 33 of them managing to survive through the entire course.

The 2000 race in Borneo brought a few innovations to the Eco-Challenge, and a record 76 teams showed up to try to outlast the others. Several standard challenges appeared throughout the course, such as trekking through rough terrain, canoeing, mountain biking, and rope climbing, but a few new disciplines were added as well. Teams had to sail through Malaysian waters, and if that didn't test their technical abilities enough, they had to scuba dive to the first ever underwater checkpoint in the history of the Eco-Challenge. Team members navigated a stunning coral reef and swam with the local sea life before completing the race. Of the 76 teams that started the race, 44 made it through to the end, with Team Salomon/Eco-Internet bringing the United States to victory once again.

The 2001 challenge is set for October, and will be held in New Zealand. 75 teams will participate through the 310-mile course in hopes of becoming the new Eco-Challenge champions.

CHOOSE YOUR OWN ADVENTURE

You might sit there watching a challenge and wonder: "Could I do that?" In fact, more and more athletes are plunging into adventure racing in the outbacks of their own states. Some compete in "sprints" that last a few hours, while others tackle races that span several days to prove they too can survive the trials of nature.

Whether they are weekend expeditions or sprints, the races incorporate similar disciplines to the longer Eco-Challenge events. Climbing, paddling, and mountain biking (the basics of which are covered in previous chapters) test your strength and stamina while you are at the mercy of the elements; at the same time navigating your way tests your judgment under these extreme conditions.

Depending on the race, equipment such as kayaks and canoes may be provided by the race organizer. Race organizers also supply maps, and sometimes will hold clinics weeks before the race so you can actually learn how to use them. Getting lost may slow you down more than injuries or fatigue.

FINDING YOUR MATES

Adventure racers rarely build teams based on brawn; more often, winning teams work well together, have complementary strengths and skills, and make good decisions as a unit. Because most adventure races are team races, one of the key elements for success is unity. Joel Geran, a member of Team Adventurefitness.com in the 2000 Borneo Eco-Challenge stresses the importance of teamwork: "You need to pick four people you can stand to be around for that long: from how they smell to their sense of humor. By day five, it's just raw emotion, and the slightest thing someone says can just tick you off. Team dynamics are an absolute if you want to finish; if you have one person who doesn't click, it'll destroy the whole group."

Of course, you may be wondering where to find other adrenaline junkies to join your trek into adventure racing. You can sometimes root out these peculiar creatures at bike clubs, running clubs, and triathlon clubs, and you can find these clubs through local bike and running shops. A few cities even have adventure racing clubs.

For many adventure racers, the Internet has been a boon for connecting with potential teammates. Geran hooked up with members of his team by posting information about himself and his racing background. When the team was formed, they met on-line and got feedback through e-mail. Training was a matter of meeting regularly in the months before the race.

TRAINING TO RACE

Preparing for a race like the Eco-Challenge can seem like a test in itself. Participants insist that anyone off the street can get ready in a year, and someone in good physical condition can probably be ready in about six months. Geran asserts, "You get a whole new perspective on how people can prepare. Some people train really hard and can't take it when they get there. Others, rookies who've never done anything like it before, get through it because they can just deal with getting beaten up for a week."

Geran often trains four to five hours a day, and goes to the gym during lunch. "I join triathlon clubs and adventure racing clubs so that I can train with people as much as possible. But when I have to do paddling or long hikes, I may not find someone, so I have to go out alone."

Training for an adventure race may seem a bit less focused than practicing for other sports. You know that you've got to be able to ride a bike, to hike, to paddle, and to read a map. Get as much information about a race as you can before you enter it. For example, find out about the terrain. Is it heavily wooded or is it marshy? The more information you get from the organizers and from past participants, the better you can prepare.

Still, race organizers may come up with any manner of madness to test your skills, so be prepared: ride horses, climb rocks, swim, and get in some target practice. Yes, that's right, target practice. You may be handed a bow and arrow, or you may be handed a rifle. You just never know.

FUNDING YOUR HABIT

You need specific equipment to participate in adventure races and the entry fees won't be cheap, so be prepared to open your wallet fairly wide for this sport. Entry fees for teams can range from more than a hundred dollars for a sprint race to thousands of dollars for an expedition-style race. You don't want to skimp on equipment, such as your bike, because faulty equipment could leave you struggling to finish.

GETTING TO THE ECO-CHALLENGE

If you can rise to the challenge of trekking hundreds of miles and fighting icy rapids to try for a purse of $100,000, entering the Eco-Challenge is not entirely out of reach. The location for the Eco-Challenge is announced at the end of the race each year and open registration for U.S. and international teams is then held in January. However, slots are awarded by lottery. In January 2000, U.S. teams for Eco-Challenge Borneo filled in one minute and international slots filled in less than two hours. The top fifteen finishers from the previous year are also invited to return.

Before you run out and try to win the Eco-Challenge sign-up lottery, there are a few rules and regulations you may need to know in order to properly prepare.

For example, the competitors are not given any specific information about the course up until the day before the race begins. They are, however, told what disciplines will be involved (such as mountain biking, horseback riding, etc.) and are required to pass a series of skills tests for the activities they'll endure.

For even more safety concerns, certain areas of the course deemed too dangerous to traverse by moonlight are considered "dark zones," and teams cannot cross such areas at night. Teams caught doing so face immediate disqualification. Also, teams must have constant visual contact with at least one fellow teammate. Furthermore, the panel of judges reserves the right to bar a competitor (and by extension, a team) from continuing due to an injury or an aggravated medical condition—with or without the consent of a doctor.

Mandatory equipment lists will vary from race to race, but based on general safety and specific disciplines to be exercised on the course, there are certain items you can count on packing along.

General safety equipment can include such things as a hand-held strobe lamp, a survival knife, survival mirror, a compass, lighter, distress flares, first aid kits, an altimeter, and a whistle. In addition, event organizers may provide a sealed radio and emergency GPS (no word on what possible penalties there are if a team unseals them).

For water courses, climbing, and other venues, equipment is provided. But as an added challenge, all equipment must be carried through the entire course or a time penalty will be assessed until the equipment is back in the team's possession, or the team will be disqualified.

Organizers emphasize the strong environmental message that goes along with the race. Three basic sets of rules go along with this philosophy. One: Pack it in, pack it out. Absolutely nothing you take into the course with you is disposable. If any traces of litter are found left behind, the guilty team is immediately disqualified from the competition. Two: Leave no trace. Teams must use trails when they're able, and when there is no trail, they cannot leave traces of one. Members are even encouraged to walk side-by-side so as not to create a new trail through the wilderness. Also, campsites must be isolated from water sources, and, again, no trace of the site is to be left behind. Campfires are strictly prohibited.

The third environmental rule requires participation in the environmental project that precedes each race. This rule extends beyond competitors to anyone involved in any way, from the race organizers to sponsors to members of the media. Basically, all these people either gather recyclable material, clean polluted areas, renovate parks and trails, or plant flora in the city or cities that host the event. Nobody can claim the Eco-Challenge isn't about getting close to nature.

THE APPEAL OF THE ADVENTURE RACE

In a mechanized world loaded with every convenience imaginable, adventure racing appeals to audacious souls who yearn to test their survival skills out in the wild world (walking through the streets of New York City may become an event soon). Joel Geran summarizes his experience with the Eco-Challenge: "Racing makes you really search inside yourself and respect the people around you. You learn that there is more to life. I look forward to the pain because it makes me feel like I'm part of the animal world." Right.

X Y Z

Xtreme Sports Photo Credits